SEARCH
AND
RESCUE
DOGS
Training Methods

SEARCH
AND
RESCUE
DOGS

Training Methods

American Rescue Dog Association

HOWELL
BOOK HOUSE
New York

Macmillan General Reference
A Simon & Schuster Macmillan Company
1633 Broadway
New York, NY 10019-6785

Maxwell Publishing Company is part of the Maxwell Communication Group of Companies.

Library of Congress Cataloging-in-Publication Data
Search and rescue dogs : training methods / American Rescue Dog
  Association.
      p. cm.
    ISBN 0-87605-733-4
    1. Search dogs—Training. 2. Rescue dogs—Training. I. American
  Rescue Dog Association.
  SF428.73.S43   1991
  636.7'0886—dc20   90-26194   CIP

10

Printed in the United States of America

This book is dedicated to:

The memory of Bill Syrotuck;
Jean Syrotuck Whittle;
the handlers and support
personnel who have contributed
so much to the American Rescue
Dog Association;
and to the dogs, without whom
none of this would have been possible.

Contents

Acknowledgments

THE American Rescue Dog Association (ARDA) wishes to express deep appreciation to Jean Syrotuck Whittle, upon whose pioneering field research and original diagrams much of this book is based, and who reviewed the entire manuscript.

The following ARDA unit members contributed significantly to the manuscript: Penny and Tim Sullivan, Emil Pelcak and Heidi Ludewig (New Jersey unit), Chuck and C. J. Melvin (Colorado unit), Tony Campion (Wisconsin unit), and Doug Stanley (Virginia unit).

We also wish to thank the following: Linda Warshaw, who provided most of the artwork; Jeff Doran, Dick Schusler and Larry Hinkle (Washington unit); Bob and Marcia Koenig (Texas unit); Don Arner (New York unit); Bev Niehaus (Wisconsin unit); Bill Squire (New Mexico unit); members of the South Dakota unit; the veterinarians who reviewed the chapter on first aid for search dogs: Bruce A. Beckmann, Douglas L. Moldoff, David Herrick and Dan Parkinson; the River Vale, New Jersey, Police Department; and Trooper Michael W. Berry, Virginia State Police Dive Team Coordinator, PADI Master Scuba Diver Trainer.

A special thanks goes to Alice Stanley for her original contributions, as well as for editing and compiling the entire manuscript.

Much of the material in Chapters 4, 5 and 6 is from Bill Syrotuck's "Training Steps for Search and Rescue Dogs," written in 1974. Bill died before he could polish the manuscript and, with the kind assistance of Jean

Syrotuck Whittle and Don Arner, publisher of *Off Lead* magazine and one of ARDA's founders, we have done so for this book.

Much of the material contained in Chapters 8 and 9 is from Bill Syrotuck's pamphlet, "The Search and Rescue Dog Unit, Part I," written in 1969.

Foreword

THIS is a book that should be of great value to dog obedience, law enforcement and canine units all over the country. It has all the ingredients on how to get the dogs in condition and start many of the necessary exercises, with step-by-step directions for following through.

It is not often that you pick up a book that covers the subject from start to finish, and as you read on you realize how demanding search and rescue is, both physically and mentally, for both trainer and dog.

The sections on search training are very well thought out and indicate that the writers have a vast amount of experience at their command and are able to share this with the reader.

A great deal of this book teaches how to read an area and what to do upon arrival at the target. It also details what is needed in the way of equipment and what can and cannot be done in various weather conditions.

The discipline used in this book is excellent. Not often does one find a book of this type painting a picture of the up side and down side of all the work involved in finding a survivor and the "on scene" care needed.

The water searching section will come as a great shock to many in the dog community. Water is a great conductor of scent and it requires a vast amount of training to help you and your dog be good at it. Rather than skipping over it due to the degree of difficulty, the authors explain water scent work.

The section on crime scene searches is also a very important element of this book, as it makes police agencies aware that civilians know what is needed to present their case. These civilians in essence are a support group for the police.

The canine first-aid section is very informative, detailed and invaluable for anyone working with dogs. Scent work is also covered, and the authors reveal how little we know of this tremendous subject that controls so much of our lives. There has been a vast amount of work accomplished here.

I have great respect for those dedicated to the art and science of search and rescue. I have but touched upon some of their techniques, however, for it takes time, patience and willingness, combined with a knowledge of how to transfer energy to a canine partner, to make the team that's needed in emergencies. Here is the handbook that is needed on "how to."

Once you start reading it, it is hard to stop. Every word and every sentence intensifies the yearning of teams to be the very best they can. May luck be their companion.

—Thomas A. Knott

Thomas A. Knott was Instructor-in-Charge of the K-9 Unit for the Baltimore Police Department, as well as Chief Instructor for K-9 Corps officers' seminars from Maine to Washington State, Alaska, the Caribbean Islands and South America. Knott also served as the White House K-9 Corps consultant, and he is an AKC approved judge for all obedience classes as well as Tracking and Tracking Dog Excellent.

Introduction

THIS book has been thirty years in the making, beginning in 1961 when Bill and Jean Syrotuck decided to train dogs for search and rescue work. The book will present much of the information contained in the files of the American Rescue Dog Association (ARDA), which was founded by the Syrotucks in 1972.

I was asked to compile the manuscript and I must admit that it was far more of an educational experience than it was work. The amount of material that the ARDA has available, both written and on tape, is awesome. The letters and notes written by Bill Syrotuck were not only fascinating reading, but they proved a history lesson in the development of the search and rescue dog program in this country. Tape recordings of ARDA board meetings in the 1970s, search critiques and training methods provided hours of listening and much material for this book.

There is far more information available than space will permit us to include. We have selected those aspects we believe to be most helpful to people seriously interested in training themselves and their dogs to be competent search and rescue specialists. We sincerely hope that all who read this text will find success in this endeavor, where trained dogs can mean the difference between life and death for a lost person.

Alice Stanley
Spotsylvania, Virginia

SEARCH
AND
RESCUE
DOGS
Training Methods

ARDA

SEARCH and RESCUE

AMERICAN RESCUE
DOG ASSOCIATION

1

Formation of the American Rescue Dog Association

IN 1961 a little girl was lost in Snohomish, Washington. The two family dogs had gone with her; one stayed but the other returned home. With some encouragement from the family, the second dog led them back to the child. Unknown to the girl or her family, this single search would have a profound effect on the search and rescue movement throughout the United States. From this incident would flow, indirectly, the development of the air-scenting search dog, the search dog unit concept and, eventually, the American Rescue Dog Association (ARDA).

Bill and Jean Syrotuck were members of the German Shepherd Dog Club of Washington State and, while their interest at the time was obedience, the lost child and the dog's role in finding her fascinated them. They decided it would be worthwhile to train their dogs to search for lost people and, with others in the club, they formed a Search Dog Committee.

In the early 1960s tracking dogs were the standard canine tool for lost-person searches, so the committee members began training their dogs to track. They felt credibility could best be gained if each dog achieved an American Kennel Club (AKC) tracking degree. When the training had progressed sufficiently, they scheduled a tracking test under a strict German judge. When they arrived at the test site, however, they found an unexpected obstacle. The entire field had been sprayed with a fertilizer containing cow

Bill Syrotuck. *Courtesy National Park Service*

manure; to make matters worse, the weather was warm and humid with stagnant air conditions. Even the dogs that managed to complete the test were marked "Failed" because they tracked with their noses far off the ground.

Hank Wilcox, a former military dog handler, had suggested that they train their dogs for air scenting rather than tracking. The fiasco at the tracking test and the realization of tracking dog limitations (due to contamination, time and weather) led the committee to heed Mr. Wilcox's suggestion. They began trying the same method to locate people he had used to search for downed aircraft during World War II. As he had trained his dog to seek the airborne scent of aircraft fuel, they would train theirs to seek airborne human scent.

TRANSITION TRAINING

The transition from tracking to air scenting was not an easy one. Handlers who had trained tracking dogs were not convinced that there might be a better way for a dog to find people. The behavior of airborne scent was a relatively unresearched factor, although military scout dogs had used this technique for years. To be successful, those committee members who believed in the concept would have to begin an extensive study and development program. Two things worked in their favor: German Shepherds proved to be natural air scenters, and the Syrotucks were both involved in scientific research that could be applied to their dog training. From the early efforts of these committee members evolved the air-scenting search dog techniques in use throughout the country today.

Among their early discoveries was the realization that dogs that were first trained to track wanted to remain "ground oriented," thereby running the risk of missing an airborne scent. Dogs that learned to air scent first would remain with that scent unless they encountered a very recent "hot" track.

After several years of training, including giving demonstrations to the local sheriff's department, the Search Dog Committee responded to its first search in July 1965. The committee was requested to search the site of a train wreck. Although all railroad personnel had been accounted for, workers reported a strong odor and the authorities wanted to ensure that a hitchhiker had not been aboard the train and buried in the wreckage.

NEW ORGANIZATIONS EMERGE

In 1969 it was decided that the Search Dog Committee should separate from the breed club. From this committee two organizations were formed: the German Shepherd Search and Rescue Dog Association (SARDA) and the German Shepherd Search Dogs of Washington State. The Syrotucks founded and led SARDA, from which would evolve the first national search dog

Jean Syrotuck Whittle.

Bill Syrotuck

organization bonded by the same training methods, standards and tests: the American Rescue Dog Association.

More training, research and refinement followed as SARDA gradually developed standards and tests for dogs and handlers. When the early evaluation tests were questioned because the weather had changed between the time a "victim" was placed and the team being tested entered the field, experienced dogs would work the test to see if the problem was with the test or with the new dog/handler team. The more experienced teams would solve the problem easily, thereby showing the validity of the test.

Each dog was required to pass five separate tests (a trail or "hasty search," open field, light brush, dense brush and a multiple-victim problem lasting several hours). After SARDA had refined these tests and put them in written form, they were adopted in 1972 as the basis for ARDA's standards. Today, they remain an accurate indication of a team's proficiency.

NEW CONCEPTS: WHAT THE DOGS TAUGHT

Since air-scenting search work was a totally new concept, training methods were tried, discarded and replaced. Among the most critical of these was motivation. The handlers found that praise alone was an insufficient reward. A stronger reward was needed and, as is so often the case, it was a dog that did the teaching.

Bill Syrotuck's dog, Randy, was an avid retriever that loved to play with a stick and was rewarded with a stick-throwing game after he found his victim. On one training problem he found the victim while out of Bill's sight and, in his enthusiasm, picked up a stick and carried it back to Bill. At that point, Bill recognized two things: play reward could serve as a training technique, and the dog could return to the handler when it had made a find. Not only did Randy show the way to the ideal reward system, but he also helped create what today is known as the *recall/refind*, where the dogs return to the handlers (recall) and lead them back to the victim (refind). The refind would prove invaluable on actual missions where the victim might be unconscious or hidden in dense underbrush, or at night when the handler's vision was greatly reduced.

While the Syrotucks felt play *might* be an excellent reward, any doubts they had were dispelled by a visit in 1971 to Lackland Air Force Base in Texas. There they saw the success Air Force handlers had in training drug dogs by using a ball or tug-of-war game as a reward. From then on, play became the standard reward in the Seattle unit and, eventually, throughout the ARDA.

Not only did the dogs respond to play eagerly, but the handlers were forced to spend more time praising the dog as it returned repeatedly with the ball or stick (sticks were preferred since one was always available in the woods). Older dogs that showed no interest in play underwent extensive "play-training" sessions at home.

Stick-play had the added benefit of increasing the indifferent dog's willingness to approach a stranger, for the dog soon learned that the stranger could be enticed into an exciting play session. This became the bond that enabled a dog to eagerly look for someone it did not know. It is a training method still valid twenty years later.

THE TEAM CONCEPT: DOG AND HANDLER UNITS

As the training for dogs and handlers was developed and refined, there also evolved the *search dog unit* concept. This was the direct result of a sheriff's complaint that, even with two Bloodhounds at his disposal, at times neither were available when he needed them. From its beginning, SARDA realized that multiple teams would mean that at least one should always be available. As they trained these multiple teams, time dictated that several handlers had to practice simultaneously, with each working problems in different areas. This training led to the realization that the same technique could be applied on actual searches. Three or more dogs deployed simultaneously could cover large areas rapidly; this could mean the difference between finding the missing person alive or dead.

A unit of multiple dog/handler teams would also need a strong support organization, comprised of highly trained base camp personnel who would maintain radio contact with handlers in the field, arrange for unit logistics and serve as liaison with the requesting agency. Today all ARDA units operate the same way, sending several dog/handler teams and base camp personnel on each search.

SARDA's reputation as a professional, successful unit grew to where they were requested to aid in searches across the country, from Alaska to Puerto Rico. Because of the professional behavior of both dogs and handlers, the Air Force Rescue and Recovery Service at Scott Air Force Base, Illinois, began flying SARDA teams to distant searches on military aircraft. The Air Force had not always experienced good results when flying dogs. There were cases of air crew members being bitten and of dogs being sick. Some crews had such negative attitudes that they would only fly dogs that were muzzled and/or crated. SARDA members adhered to these rules, but over time the friendly and professional conduct of the dogs led to a softening of the crews' attitudes. The much looser requirements seen today are a result of the exemplary behavior and training of the SARDA dogs.

THE ARDA IS FORMED

Word of the Seattle unit's work spread, both through missions around the country and articles in magazines such as the *German Shepherd Dog*

SARDA found stick play to be the ideal reward system. *Tony Campion*

SARDA responded on missions around the country, including this one to the Grand Canyon.
Bill Syrotuck

Review, published by the German Shepherd Dog Club of America. As a result, new units were formed in New Jersey (1971), New York (1971), New Mexico (1971) and Texas (1972). Along with SARDA, these units agreed to form the American Rescue Dog Association in 1972, under the guidance and tutelage of the Syrotucks. The SARDA's standards became the ARDA's standards. The new units became the beneficiaries of the Syrotucks' years of experimentation and experience.

The American Rescue Dog Association name was chosen because it implied the organization's humanitarian purpose. Technically, the dogs "search," while the handlers and other people perform the actual "rescue." However, the term *search dogs* had multiple meanings, from dogs who looked for explosives to those that sought criminals. *Rescue* immediately brought to mind a life-saving activity and the American Rescue Dog Association was, in fact, a group that performed rescues through the use of dogs.

EVALUATION SYSTEMS

Bill, Jean and others in SARDA carefully guided the new units, demanding the same high standards of those groups as they did of their own. To ensure these standards were met, they developed a membership level and evaluation system.

The first full ARDA evaluation was given to both the New York and New Jersey units in September 1977. Two members from the Seattle unit spent three days testing every aspect of the applicant unit. Each dog/handler team had to pass at least one of the five field problems, ranging from a "hasty search" along a path to one lasting three hours or more with multiple victims to be found. The unit's "specialists"—the operational leader, medical officer and communications officer—were given a battery of verbal questions and all unit members had to pass a written test covering their overall knowledge of search and rescue. Personal and unit equipment were checked to ensure that the group could handle any eventuality in the field. Handlers were picked for the physical fitness test (running three miles in thirty minutes) and dogs were put through obedience, obstacle and swimming tests.

The culmination of the evaluation centered around a mock search, where the unit was expected to perform as though on an actual mission. The operational leader conducted the necessary interviews, assessed the search problem and assigned personnel to the field. Radio communications were judged for professionalism. Base personnel were observed to see if they adequately maintained a radio log and maps showing the progress of the search, knew where the handlers were in the field, kept food and drink available and dealt appropriately with the evaluators, who role-played as the agency, family and media. Invariably, one of the "victims" required medical evacuation and the unit was assessed on its ability to treat and safely evacuate an "injured person."

After a unit had progressed to the point where it had been awarded

Provisional status and had gained even more search experience, it could request another evaluation to achieve the highest level: Full Unit. A Full Unit not only was given voting privileges on the ARDA Board of Directors, but also was declared qualified for out-of-state missions. Once achieved, however, this status did not come with a lifetime guarantee. The unit still had to pass an ARDA evaluation every three years to ensure that it was maintaining the high proficiency level required for Full Unit status. This evaluation is a severe, no-nonsense test of a unit's capabilities.

AVALANCHE AND DISASTER WORK

While Europeans had used dogs for recovery of avalanche victims since the late 1930s, the United States did not utilize dogs in this capacity until the Seattle unit began cross-training their dogs for avalanche work in the late 1960s. They found that the transfer from searching for a wilderness victim to an avalanche victim was easy for the dogs. A different command ("look for him/her") was used to cue the dog that the person was *under* the surface and to perform a much closer quartering search pattern. In 1969 a SARDA dog handled by Jean Syrotuck made the first avalanche find by an American-trained dog, on a victim buried under seven feet of snow on Mt. Rainier.

In 1969 SARDA members also became interested in training dogs for disaster work. Bill Syrotuck developed a friendship with Richard Radacovics of the Austrian Rescue Dog Brigade. This led to an exchange of visits, with Mr. Radacovics visiting Seattle in 1971 and 1972. In 1973 Bill visited Austria, Germany, Switzerland, England and Scotland to study and discuss the various aspects of avalanche and disaster techniques. Each learned from the other and, based on these discussions, SARDA devised agility and search training methods directed at preparing teams for disaster situations.

THE SEARCH AND RESCUE PIONEERS

The Syrotucks' research was not restricted to the work of search dogs. Jean, as a registered nurse, was particularly interested in wilderness medical emergencies. She was writing on hypothermia long before it became a household word. She was also concerned with the nutrition handlers needed to sustain themselves for days under the often adverse conditions of a search. Her writings became standard information disseminated to ARDA units as supplements to each member's formal first-aid training. This was especially critical in the 1970s, when volunteer search and rescue was in its infancy and standard first-aid courses offered little training on illnesses and injuries unique to the wilderness.

While Jean pursued her interest in the medical aspects, Bill became

Mapping skills of handlers are reviewed during an official ARDA evaluation.   *Penny Sullivan*

In 1973 Bill Syrotuck visited Europe and the British Isles to share training techniques.
Bill Syrotuck

intrigued by the behavior of lost persons. In an effort to determine if there was a pattern to this behavior that could aid search planners, he developed a questionnaire and began compiling statistics from various parts of the country. From this research came the first study in the field, *Analysis of Lost Person Behavior* (Arner Publications, 1976). In addition to his studies on subject behavior, Bill also began assessing search techniques used by grid (foot) searchers. The Explorer Search and Rescue Troop in Seattle was deeply committed to searching and their efforts to refine grid searching techniques aided Bill in preparing booklets on those techniques.

Bill's interest in search dogs never waned, even as he researched other areas. In 1972 he published *Scent and the Scenting Dog* (Arner Publications), which still serves as the basis for understanding, as best we can, what human scent is to the dog and how that scent is transmitted. At the time Bill was working on the book, Jean worked for the Department of Environmental Health, where she had access to a vast medical library. The material in that library, combined with her training and work in the field of dermatology, led to much of the scientific explanation of skin rafts (discarded human skin cells) and their relation to the scenting dog. A combination of scientific and in-field research by both Bill and Jean was compiled in this pioneering book, which has been translated into both German and French.

The Syrotucks' early work formed the foundation of many aspects of search and rescue as we know it today. Bill's research served as the basis for much of the material contained in search management courses offered through-out the nation. The state of Washington became the core of research on techniques to improve the missing person's chance of survival. The Explorer Scouts, the state's Emergency Services directors (Hal Foss and later Rick LaValla), Bill Wade of the National Park Service and the Syrotucks collec-tively helped change search and rescue from a disorganized walk through the woods to a sophisticated, systematic approach.

The National Association for Search and Rescue (NASAR) relied on much of Bill's work. ARDA was flourishing and needed his sure and steady guidance. In the fall of 1976, at the age of forty-six, Bill suffered a heart attack and died. He was awarded NASAR's highest honor, the Hal Foss Award, posthumously. On Bill's death, Jean became president of ARDA and it continued to grow under her leadership.

To facilitate a rapid, effective coordination system, the River Vale, New Jersey, Police Department currently serves as a round-the-clock contact. This enables any official agency to request at any time the assistance of one or more ARDA units.

Every search dog handler and every person found by those dogs owe Bill and Jean Syrotuck and the Seattle unit a tremendous debt of gratitude. This book is dedicated to them and the standards they developed. It is our hope that the information contained in the following chapters will help all those interested in search and rescue to maintain and hone the skills Bill, Jean and their team members knew were necessary to save a life.

Trained search dogs from around the country in photo taken during 1977 ARDA board meeting.
Bob Koenig

2

Before You Begin

NO ONE WILL BECOME a skilled search dog handler by reading this book alone. At some point, you will need the assistance of a skilled, experienced handler. Even when you have such help, how good you and your dog become will depend upon your dedication, the amount of time you are willing to spend and your willingness to broaden your knowledge.

Adequate first-aid training must be gained by attending local courses. Map and compass skills can be learned through joining orienteering clubs. Obedience training can be accomplished by participating in classes offered by nearby trainers or kennel clubs.

There are, however, no "local courses" available for search dog training unless a search dog unit already exists in the area. If there is one, attend a few training sessions to observe their training methods and standards. If they appear competent based on what you have read in this book, join the unit. If no unit exists or the closest one does not meet your expectations, consider forming your own. Instructors are available to present weekend seminars to potential ARDA units. Contact the American Rescue Dog Association, P. O. Box 151, Chester, New York 10918 for more information. To form a unit, you will need at least four dog/handler teams and one base camp operator. Accomplishing all the other training (first aid, map and compass, wilderness survival, etc.) will be much easier if you have a group pulling together for the same purpose.

You must be prepared to train in all kinds of weather, day and night. You must go through briers, brambles and terrain a rabbit would avoid. You must attend first aid and other classes for several hours per week in addition to your dog-training schedule. You will work, work harder and then work again. You will meet "insurmountable" problems, conquer them and meet some more. You will seem to take two steps forward, and then one step back. Your dog will appear to be a "natural," then suddenly seem to forget everything it has been taught.

You must learn to be persistent in order to overcome these problems. Persistence is an attribute search dog handlers must have. When others are ready to quit on a search, you must carry on until all probable areas have been covered. Even your dog must be persistent and willing to work in the worst weather and terrain. "Quit" is not a word in the search dog handler's vocabulary.

Your performance and that of your dog will invariably reflect your attitude. If your training is half-hearted, your dog will reflect its lack of training and enthusiasm in its lackluster attitude, looking more like it is out for a walk in the woods than actively searching ahead of its handler. If you really enjoy what you are doing, so will your dog. There is no sight more rewarding than that of a happy, eager search dog bounding ahead of its handler, obviously enjoying both the work and a strong rapport with its owner; or the experienced dog that, after eight or more hours of adverse weather and terrain, plods persistently out ahead searching the air methodically at every turn. Such teams reflect the best of search work.

You should expect the entire training process to take up to one year before you begin accepting search calls. Do not rush your training; patience will produce the best results.

Once operational and ready for actual missions, you will learn that the training was easy compared to the real thing. There is pressure—lots of it. The family is counting on you; the agency is assessing you; the media is questioning you; the victim is needing you. You are involved in a life-or-death situation.

Real missions do not wait for weekends. You must be prepared to respond immediately to any call. Can you leave work for two or three days at a time, perhaps several times a month? Can you afford to pay *all* your own expenses for both training and actual missions?

Are you afraid to go into the woods at night by yourself? How about snakes, ticks and other "residents" of the woods—afraid of them? If you have done your training properly, these dangers will make you appropriately cautious rather than unable to work.

There is no such thing as a "half-trained" handler. If you do not meet *all* the requirements, you are not mission-ready.

The decision is yours. If you would rather stay out late at a Saturday night party than worry about getting up early for a Sunday training session, search work might not be for you. If, on the other hand, this is something you have always wanted to do and you will not stop until you are good at it, you may have what it takes.

There are very few highly skilled dog/handler teams in the United States, yet the demand for their services is high. With this book, your dedication and help from some of those handlers, perhaps you, too, can become a search dog handler.

The eager search dog obviously enjoys its work.   *Dick Ness*

Several strategically located search dogs can cover large expanses of territory.

3

The Air-Scenting Search Dog and Its Selection

SEARCH TRAINING begins with the initial selection of that special dog that has the mental and physical qualities for the task, and proceeds through a great deal of specialized training. This chapter will focus on the concept of scent theory and the role it plays in search and rescue.

THE SEARCH DOG VERSUS THE TRACKING DOG

Many people think of the tracking dog as the traditional search and rescue worker, yet the tracking dog requires certain conditions be met for success:

- Scent articles are necessary so the dog can discriminate between the victim and other searchers.
- If weather or time has destroyed the physical or chemical evidence of a track, the dog cannot work.
- A single dog's reaction may adversely influence the focus of an entire search.
- It is advantageous that the area be clear of other individuals.
- Since there is a similarity of scent, other members of the family should be removed from the area.

The tracking dog is regarded as the traditional canine search and rescue tool. *Kathy Kern*

Air-scenting dog alerting on human scent, with nose held high and tail indicating its excitement.
Dick Ness

- Some tracking dogs (or their handlers) assume that if no tracks are available, then no person is in the area, which could be incorrect.
- Some starting point or known tracks of the individual usually have to be established.

If one considers the above and then looks at the scenario that follows describing the situation usually encountered on a real search, it becomes obvious that these provisions are difficult to comply with:

- Some member of the family or friends become aware of the individual being lost.
- Friends and family make a preliminary attempt to locate the individual (which means they tramp the area down).
- Others in the area are recruited to help search.
- The police are finally notified.
- A police officer is sent to the area to appraise the situation and may do some preliminary searching.
- The police officer then advises a supervisor of the situation.
- The supervisor then calls in a search and rescue unit.
- The unit arrives some time later.

Under these circumstances, much time has elapsed and the area is a physical and chemical mess, handicapping the tracking dog.

Consider now the search dog:

- It requires no scent article.
- It does not require tracks.
- The area does not have to be kept completely free of all other searchers; others can continue looking while the unit is en route.
- A starting point is not required.

There are variations and each search is different, but almost all display conditions that are more conducive to the search dog than to the tracking dog. The search dog can start off with no scent and search until it locates either a ground scent (track) or air scent. It then uses either or both to locate the lost person (preferably, it will forsake a ground scent to check out the fresher air scent). It is obvious that one search dog cannot usually do the job; it takes several and they must be strategically located.

The air-scenting search dog is based on the concept of the military "scout" dog and works in a similar manner. It alerts the handler to the presence of another individual and then must lead the handler to that individual.

SCENT THEORY

Before you can train a dog to find people, you must thoroughly understand what scent we *speculate* dogs are responding to, and the effect wind and

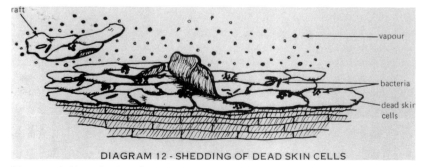

DIAGRAM 12 - SHEDDING OF DEAD SKIN CELLS

Diagram of skin cells ("rafts"), which shed at rate of about 40,000 per minute.

Jean Syrotuck Whittle

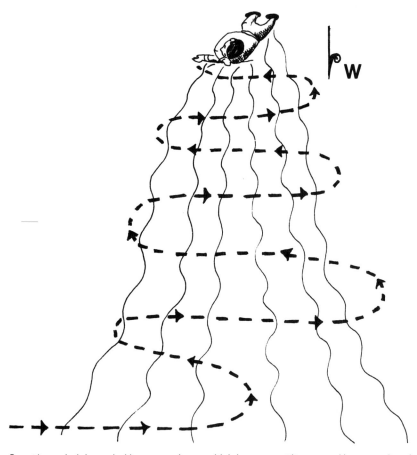

Scent is carried downwind in a cone shape, which is narrow at its source (the person) and widens with distance. Arrows indicate path dog follows as it works scent cone.

Linda Warshaw

Dog turning back into scent cone.   *Alice Stanley*

Dog alerting during brush problem.   *Emil Pelcak*

terrain have on scent transport. In the 1960s Bill and Jean Syrotuck did extensive research on airborne scent. The results were published in *Scent and the Scenting Dog* and some important points from that book will be covered here.

Humans constantly shed small cornflake-shaped dead skin cells known as *rafts*, which are discarded at the rate of about 40,000 per minute. Each raft carries bacteria and vapor representing the unique, individual scent of the person. This is the scent sought by the trained dog. These rafts are picked up and carried by air and wind currents. They are dispersed downwind in a conelike shape that is narrow and concentrated at its source (the person), but widening as the distance grows. Trained dogs can be observed literally working the cone in open fields as they zigzag back and forth, in and out of the scent.

Differing terrain and wind currents have a major impact on the dispersion of scent and each search will present its own problems. The first day of searching may be in open woods with a nice breeze; the second day may be through dense woods in hot, windless conditions. Handlers must be well versed in the effect all these factors have on scent so that they can adapt their search plan accordingly.

Terrain

Terrain features will play a role in determining how the dog is worked. Handlers in even the early stages of training must understand what effect terrain may have on scent behavior.

Open Fields. On days with a steady breeze, a trained dog should have no trouble picking up and following an airborne scent in an open field. An eager dog should alert and move in from a distance of 200 to 300 feet or more. This will be true even if the victim has been in place only a short time (fifteen to thirty minutes). A lighter breeze or very still day will also produce a good alert from a distance of 100 feet or more. Strong, gusty winds create the most problems because they can disperse the scent rapidly. Shifting winds make a search pattern difficult because you may start in what was originally a downwind direction, only to find that the wind has shifted and you are now working upwind. In such cases, the best approach is to remain with your original pattern since the wind will continue to shift and any attempt to keep up with the wind will leave you wandering aimlessly around the field.

Light Brush. Light brush is defined as a space that includes open or wooded areas with some brush or small woodpiles. Light brush problems should not pose any real difficulty for the dog as the brush should not be so thick as to block or drastically change scent flow.

Heavy Brush. Heavy brush may be found in thick woods or unmowed fields. A heavy brush area may include brier patches and large woodpiles. Still, hot days combined with heavy brush can produce extremely difficult searching conditions because the scent remains near the victim. Detection and ranging distances will be greatly reduced, thereby making relatively close sweeps of perhaps 100 feet or less necessary for accurate coverage.

Woods. Woods can vary from an open pine forest to a swamp with large trees and very dense brush. Open woods are frequently a joy to search; dense woods will try both your and the dog's patience, particularly on hot days or in the dark. The wind velocity and terrain will dictate the handler's approach to the problem. Open woods in flat terrain should not be much more difficult than an open field search. Dense woods will be similar to heavy brush problems.

Drainages. Drainages or ravines can have a definite effect on scent behavior. Since hot air rises, a drainage search during the day should be conducted along the top of the hill on the downwind side. Since cool air falls, an evening search should be conducted in the drainage itself. These search patterns will cover not only the drainage, but the slopes as well.

Drainages can also funnel scent so that it flows somewhat like a stream. If alerts are recorded in a drainage but the dog is unable to work the scent out, a careful study of terrain and airflow may reveal a funneling effect. A more thorough search can then be made of upwind areas from which the scent may be emanating.

Special Conditions

On occasion handlers will also encounter the following conditions when on a search.

Looping. Looping is sometimes found in still-wind conditions. When this occurs, the scent is carried on an updraft above the subject, transported aloft for a few hundred feet (or farther), then dropped back down. The dog will alert but then lose the scent because there is none between the subject and the point where the scent dropped. It is this situation that makes the recording of alerts so important. If one or more dogs alert in an area without making a find, that area should be rechecked on a fairly close basis. If the alert was recorded by a handler who was only halfway through a sector, however, the continuance of a normal search pattern will often resolve the problem.

Chimney Effect and Eddying. The chimney effect is the upward air flow caused by warm air (see "Drainages"). Eddying occurs along cliff walls, tree lines and similar obstructions and may disperse scent in several directions. While scent in these conditions may cause some confusion for the dog, a skilled team should have little trouble working it through. Handlers should not be so concerned with these factors that they continually alter their search plan to compensate.

Pooling. Low areas collect scent, just as they do water. As with looping, a scent pool may produce an alert that the dog cannot work to its source because of shifting winds. These alerts must be marked on both the handler's and the base maps. Handlers should assess the terrain to see what features may have funneled the scent to that particular location. When evaluating possible

Deflection of scent by downdrafts along a small drainage.　　　　*Linda Warshaw*

Looping: In still wind conditions, an updraft may carry scent aloft, transport it for some distance and then drop it back down.　　　　*Linda Warshaw*

Chimney Effect: During the day, warm air rises upslope from drainages.
Linda Warshaw

Eddying: Swirling winds along tree lines, cliffs and the like may disperse scent in several directions. *Linda Warshaw*

Pooling: Low areas collect scent just as they do water.
Linda Warshaw

origination points, bear in mind that scent can be carried for long distances before it pools. Pooling is frequently seen in the cool evening hours when the air flows downhill and may well be encountered during night hasty searches of drainages or similar terrain.

Few of the above conditions will totally defeat or deter the well-trained dog/handler team. Do not use these scent behaviors as excuses for a poor performance. To be sure, wind and terrain can combine to cause a dog to miss the victim, but such occurrences are extremely rare. Experienced handlers learn to adapt their strategy to the existing conditions and experienced dogs learn to range persistently to find the source.

As you start training your dog, you must be aware from the very beginning of wind velocity and direction, along with the effect terrain has upon this. Your dog's success will depend upon your knowledge of how to approach each problem.

SELECTION OF THE SEARCH DOG

Before choosing a particular dog, you must decide which breed you think is most suitable. When making this decision, consider the following: short-coated dogs may have trouble working in extreme heat and cold; long-haired breeds may have problems in extreme heat and are prone to brier-matted coats; short-nosed dogs generally do not have the necessary scenting ability; and sporting breeds with inbred game instinct may be more easily distracted by wildlife.

ARDA members frequently have had extensive experience with various breeds, but all agree on the suitability of the German Shepherd Dog, and ARDA members use that breed exclusively. We require that the dogs have:

- a double coat that provides protection and serves as a natural insulation for all weather extremes;
- an efficient structure that enables the dog to gait hour after hour without tiring;
- a size that is small enough to be agile and easy to transport in helicopters, etc., yet large enough to handle rough terrain;
- a high degree of intelligence and trainability;
- a proven scenting ability;
- an ability to form a strong rapport with its handler, with the resultant eager-to-please attitude critical to a successful search dog; and
- a lack of inbred game instinct, therefore making it less easily distracted by animals.

While individuals from other breeds are used for search work, we have found that German Shepherd Dogs consistently perform to these requirements.

SELECTING A PUPPY

Choosing a puppy with all the necessary mental and physical qualities is an important decision. You are not only selecting a search dog, but also a companion that will hopefully be with you for many years. There are a number of tests that can reveal certain qualities, but three things are most important: a friendly, inquisitive personality, a strong play drive and a sound physical structure.

Observing the Parents

When you observe a litter of puppies bear in mind that temperament is to a great extent inherited. If either parent or both parents are extremely shy or overly aggressive, you should consider looking elsewhere. You would be wise to observe the parents as well as the puppies in order to make a sound assessment of temperament.

A shy dog will look and act frightened, tucking its tail, looking for a place to hide or cringing behind its owner. Fear biters are pathetically terrified dogs that will, when cornered, bite their "tormentor." A puppy that flees, or whose sire and/or dam exhibit this temperament, should be immediately rejected.

Dogs may behave aggressively by virtue of natural instinct, training or abuse. Some breeders strive for dogs that show "pronounced courage," which is tested through Schutzhund, or protection, trials. These dogs generally have very sound temperaments; their aggressive behavior is carefully taught and controlled through obedience training. Puppies from such parents are usually willing to try new things and are undaunted by strange people, sounds and places.

Other aggressive dogs have owners who are very self-impressed when their dog puts on a show of "protection" by hitting the fence, barking and jumping. These dogs are rarely controlled or trained properly; many have simply been teased into acting mean. Puppies from such dogs would be far more of a risk.

The ideal parents are those that appear friendly or a bit reserved (German Shepherds are expected to be friendly but reserved toward strangers), showing no signs of either fear or aggressiveness. They will seem self-assured and content.

As you observe the parents, note how well they jump vertically (along a fence or up on a table). Strong jumpers indicate a structure that tends toward agility, and your puppy will undergo training that will require a great deal of agility.

Evaluating the Litter

Once you have seen the parents and are satisfied with their temperament, you will face one of the most challenging tasks of the aspiring search

The ARDA has found the German shepherd Dog ideal for search work. *Bill Syrotuck*

Select a puppy that exhibits a strong play drive. *Penny Sullivan*

dog handler: picking the right puppy. There they are, fluffy balls of energy and innocence, their little minds totally uncluttered—just waiting to be stuffed full with all that training. How do you choose?

Before you decide based upon what you *can* see, learn about what you *cannot* see. The breeder should be asked if the puppies have had their initial shots, worming and a health check by a veterinarian. Reputable breeders will request, or even require, that you have the pup checked by your own veterinarian within forty-eight hours of purchase. Most will place some type of guarantee on those breeds that are susceptible to hip dysplasia. This usually includes replacing the dog if it develops that disease within the first year or two. Ask the breeder if one or both parents have been X-rayed for dysplasia and, if so, whether they are listed with the Orthopedic Foundation for Animals (OFA), which rates the degree of dysplasia. A puppy with parents that were both X-rayed "normal" stands a good chance of avoiding this crippling disease.

Once you have the health matters determined, you can begin to assess the individual personalities. Generally, house-raised litters are more people-oriented than those that have spent most of their time in the kennel. House puppies have in all probability had much more socialization and play; the early experiences and stimulation of the puppies will have a profound effect on their mental development.

You want a puppy that eagerly comes to greet you. The pup that stays in the corner is showing the first signs of shyness and must be avoided. This may be the runt of the litter that has been shoved to the bottom of the pack. Some runts fight back and refuse to accept a lower station in life; these may work fine as search dogs and should not be rejected simply because they are the runt (although their smaller mature size may be a hindrance). A dog that cowers, whether runt or not, will never meet your expectations.

You do not want a bully, either—the one that "leads" the pack. Unless you are an experienced dog trainer, this dog will eventually try to test and control other dogs and even you at every turn. It may look cute and sassy now, but your amusement will wane when it reaches eighty or more pounds.

The best puppy will be the "middle child," the one that neither dominates the litter nor hides in the corner. Once you have eliminated any bully or shy ones, take the remaining pups away individually. Watch for the one that, after the initial greeting, starts to investigate the surroundings. Search dogs must be inquisitive. The puppy that curls up in your lap, while perhaps flattering, will probably be too laid back for searching. You want a puppy that shows some zest and curiosity.

Give all the remaining contenders the second important test: play drive. You will need a small ball or a rag for tug-of-war. If the puppy runs after the ball and picks it up, or gleefully grabs the rag, you have a prime candidate. If it brings the ball back to you, so much the better. If the puppy runs after the ball, picks it up and immediately drops it or simply bats at it with its paw, there is a good chance you can bring out its latent play drive. However, you should only take this play-reluctant pup if all its other qualities are outstanding.

The puppy that shows no interest in play should be rejected. A strong play drive will be critical to your final success; without it, you may never have a dog that will continue to work hour after hour, day after day, in the worst weather and terrain.

Additional Puppy Tests

Several other tests should be completed before you make your selection. The following tests will help you find the best search dog candidate.

Try to lead the puppy through tall grass. A pup that sits and cries lacks initiative. You want one that will happily follow you, tail held high in eagerness.

Make a noise by hitting a pan with a spoon or a board against a fence. Do this in a nonthreatening way (the wrong application of this test could create fear where none previously existed). The mentally sound puppy may be initially startled, but will then return to investigate. As it does so, reassure it with your voice.

Place the puppy in unusual places. Place it on a table to see how it reacts to height; walk it across a tile or cement floor to see how it reacts to unusual footing. A puppy that cannot adjust to such new experiences is probably not a good prospect.

Hold the puppy on its back for a few seconds with verbal reassurance. The ideal puppy will struggle at first, then relax and submit to your control.

If two or three pups have willingly tried and passed all the tests, let your instinct make the final choice. There will be one that, for reasons you cannot explain, seems special. You can never hope to succeed in search work without a strong rapport between you and your dog. Go with that "special one."

SELECTING AN OLDER DOG

You may already have a dog or be offered an older animal for search training. Depending upon the dog's age and background, it may be entirely suitable.

As with a puppy, you want a friendly dog that is voice responsive and exhibits a strong play drive. Many older dogs with reasonable experience among people, will be outgoing enough. The major problem usually lies in the lack of play interest if the owners did not spend much time throwing a ball or stick. Some of these dogs *can* be taught to play, but the amount of time you spend in this effort could have been better spent training the dog on search problems.

When considering an older dog, keep in mind that you will spend one year in basic training, followed by another year or two of "polishing." A three- or four-year-old dog would be five or six before it would be considered seasoned. Do you want to expend two or three years of effort on a dog with possibly two to four years of field work left, or would you be better off training a younger dog with five to seven working years ahead of it?

Insofar as gender is concerned, both males and females have shown equal ability. Choose the dog based on personality, trainability and personal preference.

Puppies must be socialized with people and other dogs at an early age. *Penny Sullivan*

4

Basic Training, Obedience and Agility

THE FIRST SIXTEEN WEEKS of a dog's life comprise a period of tremendous development. For the first twenty-one days the mental capacity of a puppy is zero. The beginning development of the senses (seeing, hearing, smelling, first emotional and social stress within the litter) occurs between the twenty-first and twenty-eighth days. At this time the puppy first starts to learn and gentle socialization is introduced.

On approximately the twenty-eighth day the brain "turns on." From the twenty-eighth to forty-ninth day the nervous system and the brain develop to adult form. The seventh week is the most critical. It is the best time for weaning from the litter and to have the puppy develop its attachment to its new master.

During the seventh to twelfth week the emphasis should be on gentle and playful introduction to early obedience (such as kindergarten puppy training). The dog's character is set by what has been learned up through the sixteenth week of life. At this time the puppy develops independence and has its first introduction to discipline.

GENERAL POINTERS ON PUPPY TRAINING

The puppy's first training starts in the home, with housebreaking being the first lesson. The owner also attempts to curb chewing. With such early lessons, the puppy "learns to learn."

A young puppy has a short attention span, thus the handlers should work only ten to fifteen minutes per session, perhaps two sessions per day. From the seventh week on you should begin socializing the puppy to interact with other dogs, other people, objects and places.

Do not use harsh corrections that may frighten the puppy, and do not use fear as a correction. For best results, use a slow but happy pace, and a vivacious, interesting voice.

EARLY TRAINING

Puppies can be started on the road to search work at the age of eight weeks. Their early life should consist of exposure to the outside world (called *socialization*) and the introduction of some degree of manners (called *tractability*). Both must be done carefully. Mishandling of either or both can quickly ruin a dog.

The overall training theme at this early age involves the dog encountering many varied situations while being guided and encouraged by its owner. This builds the pup's confidence and belief that the owner will not ask it to do anything harmful or impossible.

It learns that noises come from many sources and are both loud and soft. Moving objects have many shapes and speeds. People have many shapes, colors, smells and behaviors. A man with a cane or you with a hat at dusk may prove alarming to an inexperienced dog.

A dog that is used to trying new things with its master will not be fazed by something else new. An outstanding demonstration of this occurred when a seasoned ARDA dog and handler were working on the edge of the cement runway at Kennedy Airport. While the dog was performing the mission, a Boeing 747 came hurtling down the runway for takeoff. The huge monster passed the dog and handler just as its wheels left the ground, the wing tip passing overhead. It is difficult to imagine the immensity of the aircraft and the noise of the jet engines under these circumstances, yet the dog, confident of his handler's judgment, did not cower.

Socialization

Socialization is exposing the dog to the sights, sounds and smells of our society in such a way that the dog does not feel uncomfortable. The earlier this begins, the better. The following are some suggestions for socializing a puppy.

Car Riding. Some puppies become sick when riding in a car. The training should start with very short (ten-minute) rides two or three times a day, gradually increasing to one-hour trips.

Stay in the Car. Some puppies yell, scream and may start to tear up the upholstery when first left alone in the car. Puppies should be left in the car for

Early socialization and becoming accustomed to the outdoors will serve this young puppy well by building self-confidence and trust in the handler.

Search dogs must learn how to swim.   *Penny Sullivan*

very short periods and supervised (ten minutes). As the time is increased, supervision should become intermittent. The time should increase from ten minutes to sixty minutes. This is also a good time for the puppy to start learning the "stay" command. It has no choice, but soon associates that it cannot go with you on that command. It also becomes reassured that you always return. The puppy should learn to stay in the car even if the windows or doors are open.

It must not bark at strangers who pass by and must learn to let authorized persons into the car, including gas station attendants. The reasons for this latter training will become obvious on a search: a barking search dog does not lend comfort to the family of a missing person, and there will be occasions when the handler must ask someone to get items from the vehicle while the dog is in it.

Footing. Some puppies go to pieces on slick floors or other unstable surfaces. Pups should be exposed to surfaces that are very smooth, rough, soft, wood, cement, rocky, wobbly, uneven and moving (elevators).

Woods Walking. Pups must be acquainted with the different kinds of vegetation they must plow through on a search mission. Start with light groundcover at first, graduating to heavier and heavier brush as soon as the pup is game to try it. Exercise should include bank scrambling, little jumps, deadfall scrambling and even a careful introduction to light brambles. If the pup is responding to play with a ball or stick, that object can be used to encourage the pup to enter a small pile of brush to retrieve it.

Swimming. Swimming not only keeps the dog physically fit, but is necessary on many search missions.

Elementary Problem Solving. Predispose the pup to think for itself and to take the initiative. Some examples are: (a) learn to push open doors that are ajar; (b) run a maze that has been set up using furniture; and (c) get in and out of cardboard boxes that have the sides cut down.

Stairs. The puppy's introduction should be to nonslick, closed-back stairs. After the pup has mastered this, try open-back stairs. Be careful, however, as the pup does not watch its own footing as it sees through the steps, which appear as parallel lines.

Play. Develop a game of retrieving, using objects of different textures and sizes. Play tug-of-war and practice "give," "take it," "pull" and "out." Insist the pup release promptly when told "Give!" If it inadvertently nips you, yelp "Oww!" (which sounds like puppy language). The puppy should learn to "be gentle," "be careful." Have others play with the pup so it learns to enjoy the game with anyone. This will be critical for its later search training.

Noises. See to it that the puppy gets gradual exposure to loud noises. Introduce the pup to: the vacuum cleaner, the power mower, the rattling of pots and pans; then gradually move up to large trucks, bulldozers, car washes, etc. Be reassuring and give the pup a chance to approach and explore.

Living Things. Puppies should be familiarized with infants, children, adults and senior citizens. They should be aware of the shapes and smells of

Puppies should become accustomed to unusual footing.   *Alice Stanley*

ARDA dogs on a group sit-stay.   *Jeff Doran*

other animals: dogs, horses, cows, cats, birds, skunks, porcupines and snakes. For dangerous animals, such as porcupines, the puppy should be warned to "Leave it!" Wild animals should be identified and left alone, such as bear and deer.

Yard Behavior. Everyone wants a dog that will stay in the yard unsupervised, without tromping through the garden or digging in the petunias. Handlers should refer to several obedience books for different approaches to this. A search dog that runs loose in the neighborhood does not add credit to the unit.

Socialization should be done gradually. Do not push the pup; let it be inquisitive and learn on its own with your encouragement. If the pup is apprehensive, take the time to let it work it out or have short introductions to a particular situation with a gradual increase in exposure. Take it in the car with you to friends' homes, the park and woods, where it can be petted and played with by others. Introduce it to other puppies and dogs.

A puppy should never be placed in a position of being frightened. Do not be apprehensive yourself or your nervousness will be passed to the dog. Ensure the pup exercises some sense of caution; otherwise, it will become so insensitive that it may fall over a cliff or walk into the rotor blades of a helicopter. If you have the attitude that these environments are part of your life, the puppy will also develop that attitude.

Tractability

Tractability is the puppy's ability to try something you ask of it without being cowed or subdued. The word *obedience* does not really apply in regard to puppies less than sixteen weeks of age, even though you will be training them. Words are used, not commands. Words are associated with acts that happen accidentally or with very gentle persuasion. A seven-week-old puppy is not too young to start learning. When it is in the act of lying down because it is tired, say the word "down" in a gentle but firm voice. Furthermore, anytime it lies down for any reason, say the word "down." Praise it moderately when it has done so, but not too much for it may get up again. If you watch your dog's behavior, you will find it does all the things you want it to, on its own. It sits, stands, comes toward you, lies down, gets things, goes away from you, stays in one place or may even accidentally heel on your left side. If you attach names to these acts, the pup will soon learn what you mean, but be consistent and use the words as often as you can. You may even introduce certain positions of your arm at the same time you use the word to give the pup its first introduction to hand signals.

"No!" is a command that is overused and should be reserved only for critical situations. "Leave it," "Don't," "Hey" or "Stop" can be substituted and should be used as alternatives. If you do not want the pup to chew your favorite shoe, you can say, "Leave it!" "No" should be used for urgent situations such as chasing a chicken, chasing a car or pulling a tablecloth off a laden table. "No" in a loud, sudden voice can startle the pup into brief inaction, giving you a chance to save the dishes, etc., and follow up with, "You're not supposed to do that!" and "You leave that alone!"

Some handlers develop and use one command for life-threatening situations where, if a dog continues its actions, it may be injured or killed and it must be stopped in a split second. Single-word commands like "Stop," "Halt" or "Freeze" can be used. Upon hearing that command, the dog does not move a muscle. Teaching an instantaneous drop (down) works equally well.

In observing your puppy's actions while playing with it, you will find you can introduce it to the following words: "heel," "sit," "down," "stand," "stay," "wait," "come," "go," "take it," "fetch," "bring," "find it," "give," "out," "want to go?" and others. As the puppy grows older these words become commands, but you will find it responds to them quickly because you have done your homework. How precise its performance is will depend upon you. In search work, a crooked sit is not a penalty, but the dog must sit when told. It is not necessary for the dog to sit precisely in front of you when it is called, but it must come immediately. The measure of obedience is that the dog does what it is told without repeated commands or the necessity of yelling.

Several things should be kept in mind when working with puppies:

- Their attention span is very short.
- Their vision is not the same as humans nor at the same level.
- They are not physically able to perform for long periods or do strenuous exercises. They should be progressed in stages to match their maturing bones and muscle.

Pups must be encouraged by a happy tone of voice and made to feel that everything is fun, fun, fun—with only occasional moments of dead seriousness. Obedience work can be seriously mismanaged, producing a dog that will not take any initiative for fear of reprimand. Search dogs are not machines; they do not repeat the same set of exercises for the highest score. They must often use their own initiative and talent to solve problems since they are seldom in the same situation twice and no two missions are the same in either circumstance or environment.

OBEDIENCE

Even though your dog is the "model of the neighborhood," you should plan to take it to regular obedience classes.

Advantages of Additional Training

Your formalized training with the dog is somewhat sporadic. These classes will put you on a schedule with weekly deadlines and the need for regular practice. This will produce a good working relationship between the two of you.

Such classes will expose you both to other dogs in a new environment. There is absolutely no substitute for the commotion and distraction of an obedience class. Your dog will learn to improve its attention to you in the midst of confusion.

By aiming for top performance and precision you will improve your teamwork with your dog. You will find you enjoy doing a good job and you are bound to learn some new training ideas.

You will also learn a great deal about dog behavior in general by watching other people handle their dogs. This will prove valuable when you later want to teach your dog something unusual.

Since there are many excellent books available on obedience training, precise methods will not be presented in this text. However, all dogs must learn the following basic obedience skills: heeling (on and off leash), recall (come), drop on recall (to be able to stop a dog instantly) and sit-stay and down-stay.

Specialized Skills

In addition, search dogs require specialized obedience training. ARDA standards require the dogs to pass tests on the following skills. These tests ensure that all dogs are obedient and calm under the wide variety of distractions and conditions encountered on searches.

Response to Another Handler. The dog must heel, on lead, with another unit member.

High Jump. The dog must jump into the back of a pickup truck or equivalent, to a height of about thirty-six inches (this is often required for transport at search sites).

Dog Behavior. Four dogs will be loaded into the back of a pickup truck and then transferred by a handler, one dog at a time, on or off lead, to the back of a second pickup truck parked about twenty-five feet away. After all the dogs are transferred, the handler will move to a position about fifty feet away and, in sight of the dogs, fire a starter pistol or pen-gun flare. The dogs must remain calm and quiet at all times.

People Acceptance. While the dogs are in the truck after the preceding test, three strangers will come to the truck, pat and talk to each dog. The dogs should show neither aggressive nor shy behavior.

Vehicle Behavior. With the dog in the handler's vehicle, three strangers will one at a time pass within one or two feet of the vehicle, drop an object, pick it up and move on. They will make no aggressive moves, touch the vehicle or talk to the dog. The dog must remain calm and quiet.

Retrieve in Water. The handler will throw an object forty to sixty feet out into the water. On command, the dog will retrieve and present the object to the handler. The object of this test is to assess water entry, competent swimming and retrieving.

A well-trained dog will jump anything. . . or anyone.   *Bill Syrotuck*

ARDA unit practices group heeling exercise.   *Todd Reinertsen*

Long Down. Four dogs, on lead, will be put down in a circle ten feet in diameter. They will stay in that location for a period of fifty minutes under the supervision of one handler, with handlers to change every ten minutes. The dogs may shift, sit up and go down again, but must remain in the same location. This exercise is to practice for situations when one handler must watch all unit dogs while other handlers are eating or otherwise occupied.

Transportation. Four dogs will be loaded in the back of a truck and transported over a dirt road, with handlers present. This test simulates transport situations frequently encountered on actual missions.

Directed Search. The handler will send the dog out by voice and/or hand signal a minimum distance of fifty feet to search a particular area.

Confinement. The dog is put in a very confined space, such as on the floor of the front seat of a car, beneath the handler's legs. The dog must show a willingness to be confined.

Control. The dog and handler will walk single file in a line of other people and dogs along a narrow trail with the dog showing good behavior on a loose lead.

AGILITY

Agility training serves two purposes: it gives the dogs confidence in themselves and their handlers, and teaches the dogs to handle unstable or difficult footing. Agility training is normally achieved through the use of an obstacle course, which may include various types of ramps, planks, ladders, jumps and tunnels.

Obstacles

All ARDA dogs undergo extensive agility training. Most units have created their own courses with a wide variety of obstacles.

Fifty-five-Gallon Oil Drums. When the ends are removed, these drums can be used as tunnels, particularly for young dogs since the height and circumference is less intimidating than a smaller space. They can also serve as an unstable surface for the older dog to jump up on or climb over.

Ramps. Ramps may be made from wooden planks that are either smooth or equipped with "cheaters" (small boards nailed crosswise to provide a grip for the dog). Cheaters should be used for young dogs, but older dogs must eventually be able to climb a ramp without them.

Jumps. These may be bar jumps (a single board or rod suspended between two posts); broad jumps, which require a dog to jump *across* rather than *over;* a six-foot piece of plywood that the dog must scramble up and over; or a solid "wall" jump that is adjustable in height. Be sure the jump will "give," or fall, if the dog should hit it.

Unit dogs quietly accept being loaded in one vehicle.   *Don Arner*

The long-down exercise required of ARDA dogs.   *Donna Hreniuk*

44

A multiple-use obstacle with ladder, platform, ramp and "climb-through" tire.

Doug Stanley

Dogs should learn to come down ladders slowly, rather than jump off. *Jeff Doran*

Handlers should start demanding sits and stays on stable portions of the obstacle course.

Emil Pelcak

Puppies should be introduced to obstacles gently, using a favorite toy as an enticement.

Bob Snyder

Metal Highway Culvert Pipes. Not only do these make excellent tunnels, but you may actually have to send the dog through one independently during a search (small children may hide in them).

Teeter-totter. Walking on a teeter-totter teaches the dog to handle extremely unstable footing. It may consist of nothing more than a wide plank nailed to a round log.

Platform. This may be a relatively small, square board placed at a height of about thirty-six inches for training the dog to jump vertically. A platform may also be used in combination with a ramp.

Ladder. Ladder climbing should not be attempted until the dog is confident in stair climbing. A ladder can be extremely difficult for the dog since it is not only open backed, but also more vertical than most stairs. It may be used in conjunction with a platform so that the dog has somewhere to go when it reaches the top of the ladder. A child's slide at a playground serves this purpose well.

There are many other obstacles or variations of those described above that can be created with a little imagination and a minimal amount of carpentry. A well-planned obstacle course not only trains the dog to handle a variety of situations, but also can provide an exciting and fun challenge for both dogs and handlers.

Training for Obstacle Work

Dogs that exhibit an eager-to-please attitude will show a willingness to try any obstacle the handlers ask of them. Dogs that possess such an attitude as well as a strong play drive will be undaunted by the unusual footing they may find on both wilderness and disaster missions.

The play drive can be used as motivation for agility work, just as it is for search training. As the dog completes each obstacle, reward it with its favorite toy or stick. Eventually, you can withhold play until the dog has completed the entire course. Using this method, handlers will find they have a dog that will complete the entire course, off leash, with enthusiasm. One of the easiest ways to build the fun and excitement is to work in a group with other dogs, especially with those experienced and confident on the various obstacles.

Safety is imperative and you must always work with one or more assistants if the obstacles are very high or possibly dangerous. *Always ensure success.* If a dog is having trouble, suspend training on that particular obstacle for a day or two and then try again. End each session with several obstacles that the dog loves to work and on which it particularly excels.

While working obstacles, the dogs should learn a variety of commands. When asked to climb something, they should be told to "Go on up" or "Hup"; when entering a tunnel, "Go on through" can be used. Use words or phrases that make sense to *you* so that you can be consistent in their use. To prevent the dog from becoming too fast or simply performing the course

A large dog obeys command to go through a small pipe.
Alice Stanley

Dogs should become accustomed to being raised in a front-end loader.　　　*Alice Stanley*

by rote, alternate your approach to each obstacle or occasionally require the dog to come back over or through one it has just completed.

Once the dog feels comfortable and confident on the various obstacles, the handler may caution the dog to move more slowly using the "easy" command in a low, drawn-out tone. The handler should also start demanding sits, downs and waits on the stable sections of the course. A careful turn around command and directed rights, lefts, ups and downs to various prominent obstacles and levels from some distance are also useful.

Puppies should be started on a small, nonthreatening course. A wide board with each end resting on a cinder block laid on its side makes an excellent beginner's plank. Any jumps should be only inches off the ground to avoid undue stress on still-developing bones and muscles. A very easygoing, gentle approach, combined with play reward, will produce a puppy that will anticipate this "new game."

Progress slowly. Properly done, agility training will greatly increase the dog's confidence. Do not test or proof the dog on flimsy material that may give or break under the dog's weight. Such difficult obstacles should only be attempted when the dog is thoroughly trained and even then it should be done cautiously.

At times it will be necessary for the handler or others to physically assist the dog by grasping the scruff of the neck, etc. As part of agility training, the dog should become accustomed to being pushed, pulled and lifted from various angles.

If available, a tractor with a front-end loader or similar equipment should be used to lift the dogs and handlers. This training not only requires trust between the dogs and handlers, but also prepares them for any situation where they may have to be lifted up on a rubble pile during a disaster mission.

Good agility and obedience training will pay dividends when the team must work in rugged terrain or on a disaster search. It will also develop mutual respect and confidence between dog and handler.

An eager search dog bounds ahead of handler as she gives strong verbal encouragement.

Bill Syrotuck

5

Beginning Search Training

$\mathbf{A}$S YOU BEGIN your training you will want to determine your progress. What do you do next? Are you going too fast? Without some yardstick, it is difficult to tell. We have put the training into steps to make it easier. Your progress will depend upon your ability and knowledge, your dog's ability and knowledge and on the time you are willing to invest. Training five times a week for three weeks amounts to fifteen sessions. If you train only once a week, it will take more than three months to cover the same ground. It may take even longer, as the dog will tend to forget some of its training from one week to the next.

Do not start search training until you have had the dog or puppy for at least one week and have spent that week playing with it and firmly establishing that you are its master and friend. The dog's initiative to find you will depend upon its attachment to you, and this is where it all begins. For purposes of brevity, we will assume you are starting with a puppy.

As you start your training, you should use a particular collar or leash so the puppy will become "cued" as soon as that equipment is brought out.

STEP 1: THE RUNAWAY GAME

Note: Step 1 is for very young puppies only; older dogs should start with Step 2.

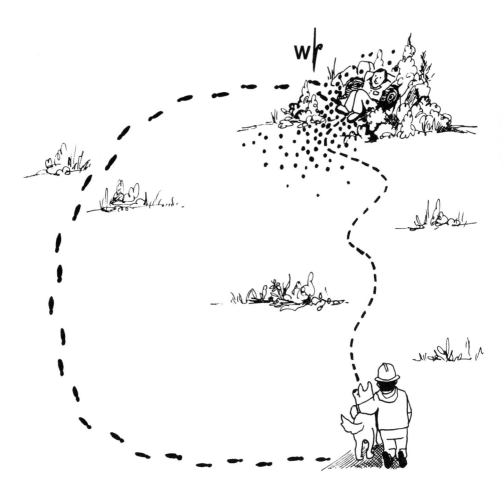

Beginning search problem: "Footprints" denote route taken by "victim"; dotted line is that normally taken by dog.　　　　　　　　　　　　　　　　　*Linda Warshaw*

Choose open areas that are relatively flat with small clumps of cover, grass, shrubs or weeds. Select a time of day that is not too hot or bitterly cold. Check that there is a light breeze blowing and know the direction of the wind.

Since the puppy is very small (eight to ten weeks of age), you can generally outrun it. This exercise can be done without the aid of an assistant.

1. On arrival at the area, allow the puppy a few minutes to acquaint itself with the grass, smells, noises, etc.
2. Start walking slowly with the pup to establish its attention and have it moving along in your direction.
3. When you have its complete attention, quickly run ahead of it, into the wind, and call, "Here boy! Puppy! Puppy! Puppy!" Use an exciting manner and voice.
4. When you have outdistanced the pup by 50 to 100 feet, flop down behind a clump of grass (out of its sight) and wait for its arrival.
   (a) If the pup does not come straight to you, give it a few moments to see if it can discover you with its nose.
   (b) If it looks stumped or confused, make a sound or motion to attract it.
5. When the pup discovers you, lavish it with praise and a play session (even very young puppies may grab a squeaky toy and such interest should be encouraged from the very beginning).
6. Avoid startling the pup when it finds you. Many puppies temporarily freeze when they see their master in an unusual position and location (lying down in the grass). Speaking to them is usually all that is necessary to reassure them.
7. Repeat the runaway game two more times immediately.

Remember that a puppy is like a baby. Once you disappear, you are "really" gone and it will be unable to remember exactly where you are. If you have planned the wind properly, it will soon discover you by using its nose. Dogs see motion much better than detail so, if you remain frozen, the puppy will not notice you even if part of you is exposed.

By using the same area over and over for the exercises, the pup will start to associate the area with the game and become cued upon arrival.

Variations

Run in a small arc so that the pup will try to shortcut the last part and will start to rely on its nose and the airborne scent.

Change areas occasionally. As the pup gets better, include areas with small ground cover.

Schedule

1. Two to three times each outing.
2. Several outings in close succession (not more than ten times total).

Transfer to Step 2 as soon as possible.

The runaway problem:
Step 1: The owner entices pup with stick, then runs in a semicircle while assistant excites the dog.

Step 2: The pup is released and races to owner, with the assistant following behind giving verbal encouragement.

Step 3: The owner rewards the puppy with a play session.   *Tim Sullivan*

STEP 2:   TRAINING WITH VISUAL CUES

This is also frequently referred to as "runaway training." Use an assistant who thoroughly understands what you are going to do. A family member is most handy, but sometimes a pup is too content to stay with them instead of running after you. If Step 1 has become a great game, leaving the pup with the assistant so that both of them come after you should not pose a problem.

Go to the usual working field. Have the assistant hold the pup by placing one arm around its body and the other hooked through the collar. If you are using a choke collar, do not hold the ring as this will tighten the collar into a correctional hold. You want to *contain* the pup, not correct it.

The master talks to the pup in an enticing and exciting voice, and augments this with hand clapping or showing the puppy its favorite toy. While still talking and calling to the pup, the master runs away in a semicircular path and drops behind a bush or clump of grass about 100 feet upwind.

As the master leaves, the assistant helps increase the pup's curiosity and excitement by saying, "Watch him! Where's he going? Look at that!" (Do *not* say "Find him!" until the moment the pup is released.) While containing the puppy, the assistant must permit enough freedom of movement to allow the pup to hop around in eagerness. As the master disappears (by diving behind a bush), the assistant makes sure the pup sees where the master has vanished and immediately releases the pup with the urging to "Find him!" The release is best done at the point when the pup is straining in an effort to follow the master. The assistant follows the puppy and calls out, "Find him! Atta girl! Find him!"

If the pup stops in confusion, the assistant also stops and allows the puppy a chance to find the scent on its own. If this is unsuccessful, have the master call out. Repeat if necessary until the pup alerts and starts to "home in," then stop calling.

Lavish the pup with praise and/or play from both the master and the assistant as soon as the find is made. Do not stand around talking about any problem; the puppy must be rewarded *immediately*.

Repeat, right away, two more times, being sure that the exercise is into the wind.

Reminders

The dog can be taken to the area on lead, but never on a heel command. This would constitute a form of constraint when the goal of beginning searching is maximum freedom, motivation and speed.

Never tell the dog to "stay" with the assistant. You *want* it to fuss to be released. "Stay" is used when you want the dog to be quiet and controlled.

Never use "come" as an enticement. This is a command you want to reinforce by having the pup come immediately and, obviously, the assistant will not let that happen. Older dogs may decide to take a nip at the person who will not let them go once they hear the "come" command.

The problem must be set up so that the puppy will leap forward toward the last visual location of the master. This shortcuts the ground trail and encourages the dog to use air scent alone to complete the problem. If the dog finds the trail and elects to follow it at some point, allow it to do so. Try to set the next exercise with a wider semicircle so as to avoid trailing.

Use words of encouragement when the pup's head is held high and it is using the air currents.

When a dog trails or tracks at this stage, *never* correct or reprimand it. You have asked it to find the person by using its nose and you must allow the pup to do this the best way it knows how. It is up to the master to be smart enough to set the problem up in such a fashion that air scenting is the quickest and easiest way for the pup to solve it.

The pup *must always* succeed and make the "find."

Both the master and assistant must reflect great excitement and enthusiasm in their voices. One of the most difficult things for new handlers to learn is proper voice inflection. There is no room for shyness when you are trying to stimulate a dog's eagerness.

Variations

As soon as the pup is responding well and running out eagerly, start to decrease the calling while you run away. Tantalize the puppy as you leave, but not after.

Introduce a tug-of-war rag, a stick or a ball to bait the pup as you are leaving. Praise the pup and play with the object when the "victim" gets found.

Increase and vary the distance from 100 to 500 feet. Vary the number of problems per outing from one to three.

Once the dog has a good understanding of the game and has a reliable, eager response, try a "check mark" problem. Run in a semicircle, as before, until you are about 100 feet away, then stop and face the pup. At this point, the assistant will turn the pup so it cannot see you. Walk about 25 feet back toward the pup, but off to one side of the path you have run. Be sure the wind is *behind* you as you drop down in the grass or behind a bush. As soon as you are down, the assistant will turn the pup back in your direction and release it on the "find" command. The puppy should hit your airborne scent before it gets to where it last saw you because the scent will be blowing from you across its path.

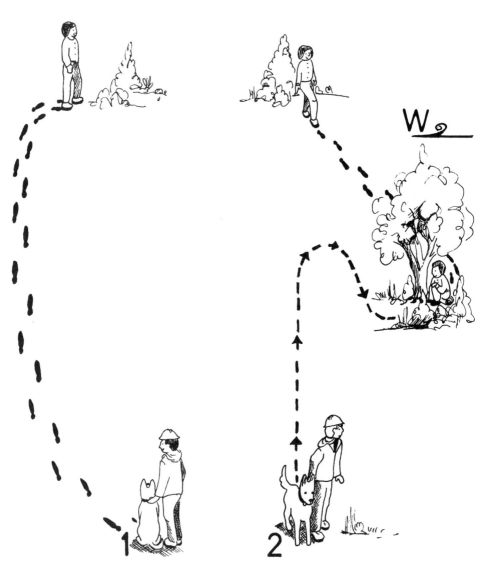

W

1

2

Checkmark problem: After handler runs in semicircle (1), assistant turns dog while handler moves back into wind and hides (2). Dog is then turned around and released on "find" command.

Linda Warshaw

Schedule

1. One to three times each outing.
2. Three to five times a week.
3. Practice for two weeks.

The dog knows Step 2 well when it whines and squeaks with anticipation and races out after release with no hesitation or uncertainty. In a breeze of five to ten miles per hour, it should be able to "home in" on the master in an almost straight line.

STEP 3: INCREASING TIME AND DIFFICULTY

This is the step where you want to introduce other people and increase the working time and difficulty. You are preparing for Step 4, where the dog will learn to look for a "victim" *without* seeing that person leave.

The first stranger or other person for the pup to find should be a good acquaintance of the dog or a member of the family. Ideally, it should be someone with natural exuberance who likes and enjoys animals. This person should be willing to spend time playing games of tug-of-war or chase the stick with the pup and not be shy about sounding excited while doing so. This game-playing reward cannot be overemphasized. Initially, lavish praise and rolling and tumbling are very adequate rewards, but this can eventually become a "so what" situation unless the pup finds that strangers can be finagled into all kinds of fun things. This is an important part of its basic attitude toward all strangers.

During this step you will alternately use a friendly acquaintance and yourself as victims. Use other people for search problems as long as the dog performs well. Insert yourself as the victim each time you try something different or difficult.

Use yourself as the victim to try the following:

1. Change to slightly denser brush.
2. Make the pup wait three to five minutes before starting after you. Try leaving it inside the car (with supervision from the outside) where it can watch you leave after you have said a very intriguing good-bye. You should still make a running departure because it is the best attention-getting device. You can slow down to a brisk stride for some of the easier problems done in open terrain. Be sure the dog notices you near your end point, or it may try to trail; if necessary, call out to it.
3. Scramble up rock piles, steep banks, piles of dead trees or log jams. You lead the way and get the pup to scramble after you. It has to learn where to place its four feet compared to your two, and this will take some doing. With experience and familiarity, the dog will show

The puppy must learn to scramble up difficult footing, such as this
pile of logs. *Todd Reinertsen*

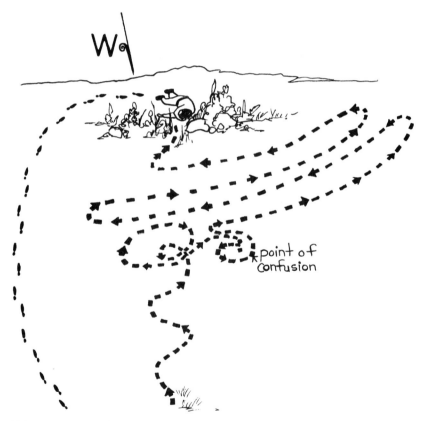

point of
confusion

If the dog seems confused, handler should move closer to victim and begin semicircular
sweeps until dog hits scent. *Linda Warshaw*

quick improvement and eventually you can throw a stick or favorite toy into the middle of such a pile and have it happily scramble after it. Be sure to remove the choke chain or training collar for this type of exercise to avoid any possible entanglement.

4. Try some tall brush with a good wind sweep through it, but without much deadfall. Have the assistant alert the dog with a "listen" command. Be sure the victim (you) steps on lots of twigs or makes enough noise for the dog to cue on. Again, use the basic semicircle pattern into the wind.

Use friends or family as the victims in these exercises:

1. Start with a short, easy field problem with the victim first tantalizing and enticing the pup, then running away as per the beginning of Step 2. Cue the dog with "Watch Jim! Where's he going?" Upon release, say "Find him! Find Jim!" Dogs can and should learn the names of family, friends and other handlers and this is a good way to start.
2. As the dog responds and performs well, increase the distance and working time, as in Step 2.
3. Have the victim bait the dog with a stick or tug-of-war rag as soon as the pup will respond to this game. Always use it as a reward. Discover and use whatever is a "turn-on" for the dog.
4. If the puppy is responding very well, then use your dog's favorite friendly victim and try a light brush problem.

Reminders

If possible, use the same acquaintance until the dog has progressed noticeably and responds with maximum eagerness. You can then try one other person and alternate between the two, identifying each by name to the dog.

If at any point the dog is unable to close in on the victim, work it in a semicircle around the downwind perimeter until the dog reacts to the scent. Immediately reinforce the response with "Atta girl! That's it! Find him! There he is!" *The dog must always succeed*, even if you have to walk it over to the victim (never do so in a straight-line pattern).

Schedule

1. Two to three times in each session.
2. Three to five times a week is most preferred.
3. Practice for eight to ten weeks.

A mature dog with a strong play drive and very good handler rapport should progress rapidly through the first three steps.

STEP 4:   TRANSFER TO NONVISUAL CUES

This is the lead-in to basic search work. Once you and the dog have mastered this step, the possibilities are unlimited. There are six exercises in this step.

1. Go to the usual working field with your assistant. Have the assistant let you out of the car at Point A and then drive the dog to Point B. The assistant then removes the dog from the car, being careful not to reprimand it for eagerness or exuberance, yet still keeping good control. If the dog gets loose at this point, the owner should hide immediately and let the dog complete the problem.

   The dog and assistant move to a location where they can watch the owner walk from Point A to Point C and disappear. The assistant alerts the dog with "Watch him! Where's he going?" The owner may have to wave his arms or call out briefly to attract the dog's attention.

   The assistant releases the dog with "Find him!" and helps to get the dog into a good downwind position if the dog has any difficulty. As a last resort, the master can call out once or clap his hands. If the dog requires some assistance from the victim, let it complete the problem without further assistance when possible. Encourage the dog, but avoid a constant stream of chatter. Remember to reward generously; do not shortchange the praise and play while the two of you discuss the performance.

2. If the first exercise worked well, repeat again in the same locale. Do not let the dog see the owner hide this time. The sound cue is optional.

3. Repeat a third time, using no sound cues if possible. If you have any problem in the previous exercises, continue to use the sound cues for one or two days, until the dog has it mastered, then move on to the next exercise.

4. Use your friend (assistant) as the victim and repeat the first three exercises on your next working session. Again strive for minimal to no cues except to let the dog know that you have let someone out of the car to go hide.

5. Place the friend (victim) in the usual search area without the dog's knowledge. About fifteen minutes later, go to the area and work the problem. The object is to keep working the dog back and forth across the wind (eventually through the scent cone) until it notices and alerts. Keep the first problem relatively short, perhaps five or ten minutes in good wind conditions. Do not let the dog lead you aimlessly through the area; decide upon your search pattern, based on wind direction, and stick with it. Break your pattern only when you know the dog has picked up and is working the victim's scent (you

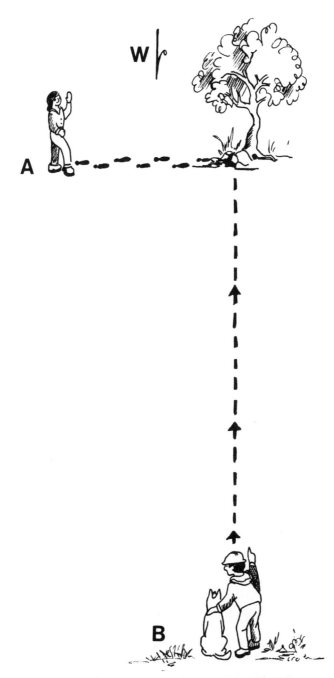

"Point A to B" problem: "Victim" is dropped off at Point A and dog is taken to Point B; dog watches person walk across and hide as handler provides verbal excitement. Dog is then released on "find" command.   *Linda Warshaw*

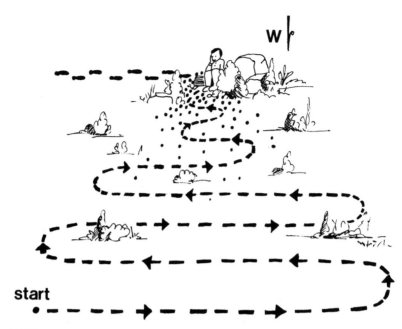

Gridding an area across the wind until the dog intersects the scent cone and closes
in. *Linda Warshaw*

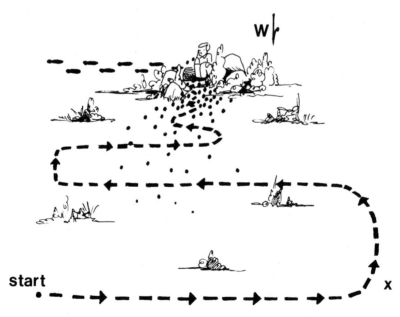

Shortcut method of gridding if dog seems confused: Handler recognizes at Point X dog
is not working properly and moves closer to "victim" to begin sweeps. *Linda Warshaw*

must know exactly where the victim is at this stage of training). Be encouraging and watch the dog like a hawk. The moment it shows an alert, encourage it with "That's it!" When it starts to move along the scent cone toward the victim, continue to encourage it with "Atta girl! Good girl! Find him!"

If the dog appears uncertain, cut the problem short by moving in closer to the source of the scent so that the dog can pick up on it during the first or second pass.

6. Introduce the dog to the use of the scent article. Use a tennis shoe, sock or T-shirt of the victim.

As you give the command "Find Jim!" offer the scent article about one inch from the dog's nose. If the dog wishes, let it mouth or sniff the article for up to five seconds, saying, "That's Jim, let's find Jim!" If the dog is not particularly interested, *do not* force the article on it. If the article is in a bag, do not force the dog's head in the bag!

Any time the dog returns to you during the exercise, offer the scent article for a quick whiff. Again, do not insist or force it. Often a dog will recognize "Jim's" scent when you first offer the article and will need little reinforcement. Eventually the dog will realize this scent belongs to the person it should be looking for.

Reminders

Never move in a straight line toward the victim. If at any time the dog is bored or the problems are not working well, drop back to an earlier stage, with variations, where the dog was performing successfully.

Variations

Do longer problems in open terrain. Increase the total distance as well as the number of passes.

Try light brush problems with a good breeze blowing. Use other members of the family as the victim. Use the scent article on alternate problems.

If the dog lacks eagerness, displays uncertainty on the close-in or lacks willingness to work, spend more time on motivation by game-playing with the victim or use a family member as the victim.

Scent Articles

The following articles are recommended for scent work:

- Unlaundered items worn next to the skin (T-shirt, socks, pillowcases or a clean rag worn under a shirt for several hours).

- Well-worn items that do not get laundered frequently, such as stocking hats, gloves or tennis shoes.
- Less desirable items that are awkward to carry include jackets, coats or trousers.
- If the article accidentally gets handled for a few moments by "other people," this should not affect its use. If there is any doubt as to the validity of the article (it "might" belong to someone else), *do not use it*.

Schedule

1. Three short problems each session.
2. Three times a week.
3. Practice for one week.
4. Progress to three medium to long problems (fifteen to thirty minutes) per session, three times a week.
5. Practice medium to long problems for two weeks.

The dog is ready for Step 5 (see Chapter 6) when:

1. It understands when you get to the area and give the "find" command that there is a victim there even when it has not seen or heard the victim being placed.
2. It will keep searching and moving out ahead of you for the full thirty minutes.
3. It closes in on the victim from a distance of 90 to 150 feet in a good breeze.
4. Its close-in is both certain and eager 90 percent of the time.

Dog being given a scent article. *Penny Sullivan*

6

Advanced Search Training

THIS CHAPTER contains training methods intended to increase the working scope of the dog. The basic search problems presented in Steps 1–4 in Chapter 5 will be continued, with increasing variations.

STEP 5:   IMPROVING SEARCH SKILLS

Practicing the following variations will help enhance your dog's search skills:

1. Increase and vary the dog's working time from thirty minutes to two hours; insert ten-minute problems occasionally to keep the dog's motivation high.
2. Increase the working area up to one-half square mile or a narrower area approximately one mile long with the victim at the far end.
3. Vary the terrain. Use a mixture of light to medium to heavy brush. Start the heavy brush as somewhat shorter problems with maximum motivation.
4. Start working short, easy problems in "contaminated" areas where you know other animals and people have recently been. Try a second problem in the same area a short time later. Be prepared to watch the dog and learn something yourself. Be prepared to assist the dog slightly.

The polished dog works independently through rough terrain.   *Bill Squire*

5. Start using a complete stranger occasionally for short problems, but use a scent article.
6. Do several problems where the victim's exact location is unknown to you.
7. Start using two victims occasionally. Begin with short problems, approximately ten minutes to find victim A, stop and praise, then move on to find victim B. Gradually increase the time to approximately thirty minutes each.

At this point in training, it is often obvious if you have a dog that works either too fast or too slow. This will vary according to the dog's personality and is somewhat affected by your basic training technique. At any rate, you will probably want to speed the dog up or slow it down.

Slowing Down

With a dog that is voice conscious (yours should be), often all you have to do is give the command "Dusty, wait." Calling the dog's name tends to make it start back to you. As soon as the dog is where you want it, send it again with, "Okay, Dusty, let's *find* Joe!"

Practice the "wait" command when out walking the dog, especially along trails or during obstacle course work.

If you have an especially exuberant dog that is frequently out of sight in brush, call "Bruno, wait!" and duck into the nearest good hiding place. Be prepared to wait for your dog to discover you are missing and come back to find you. When it does, say "Good dog! Let's go find!" and start searching again. Repeat this several times, about ten minutes apart, and your dog will soon start looking over its shoulder to make sure you are still there. If the dog ranges too far, its sense of responsibility will bring it back periodically to check on you. This technique should produce a working pattern where the dog ranges out in large circles that loop back to the handler.

Speeding Up

Some slow dogs spend too much time sniffing out the whole environment. While this is interesting, it is not why you are out there. Allow the dog to check out the basic smell of the area for a few minutes before you start working. When it starts sniffing clumps of grass, cow pies or the area around trees, this constitutes plain "dinking around." You do not want to turn them off to all scents in the area because a dropped glove may get ignored. Allow one quick sniff followed by "Okay, let's go!" or "Leave it, let's find Linda!" or, if the dog is behind you, "Come on, let's go find her!" You should move out at a brisk pace. If you leave the dog behind, call out "Jory, get up here—let's go!" As soon as Jory moves ahead of you, praise him with "Atta boy! Let's go find Linda!"

Young dogs and sometimes older ones can be "turned on" by having to observe other eager workers do a short problem, while they must wait and watch from a distance.

The slow dog may need to drop back to some easier problems and work more on game playing. Dinking around generally indicates a lack of enthusiasm for the task at hand, which in turn indicates a lack of sufficient motivation.

You may have a dog that works perfectly well in front of you (is eager and trying), but does not get quite as far out as you would like. To increase its ranging, face in one direction and start off eagerly, telling the dog "Let's find John!" As the dog races out ahead of you, move only a short distance, then veer back in the opposite direction. As the dog comes racing back toward you, send it off again with "Atta boy! Find John!" Again, as your dog speeds out, go only a short way and then veer back to your original direction of travel.

If you use an arm signal as you send the dog out, you will soon develop a method of directed sending that will prove handy when you want to send the dog to check out a particular area. This is similar to a technique known as directed retrieving, which is used for bird dogs. During directed searching you run the risk of the dog listening so hard for the change of direction that it is not paying attention with its nose. To avoid this, use these commands on an informal and occasional basis.

Sometimes a slow dog is the product of a slow, unenthusiastic handler. Learn to use an eager tone of voice and a brisk pace to set the working tone at the start. Do not slow your pace to stay behind the dog; if it is moving slowly and you speed up, it will also quicken its pace. A dog that is moving out at a good clip is less likely to dink around. Learn to use tones of voice to good advantage. *Do not* say, "Come on, let's go find him!" To the well-trained dog, "come" means "return to me"; thus, you are giving off conflicting commands.

Sometimes a dog is a little slow because it has been given too much play time, tearing around and using up all its spare energy and interest before working the problem. Play should come *after* the work session.

Reminders

If the dog really messes up, analyze the situation. This is how a handler learns. The odds are that you made a judgment error (the victim was not where you thought or the wind was not as strong as you thought). If you appraise it properly, you may recall that the dog indicated "something," but you failed to recognize it or you did not follow up.

Never reprimand or punish the dog, no matter how badly it may have worked. Punishment will quickly cause the dog to look busy for the sake of looking busy. There it is, sniffing up a storm and not even trying to find the victim. You will never know the difference until it is too late. Remember you can *train* the dog to use its nose, but you cannot *force* it; the dog must enjoy its job if it is to eventually work long hours in adverse conditions. If the dog

An advanced dog should range ahead of its handler, seeking the airborne human scent.

Jean Syrotuck Whittle

The ranging dog should loop back to its handler.

Courtesy Virginia Department of Emergency Services

71

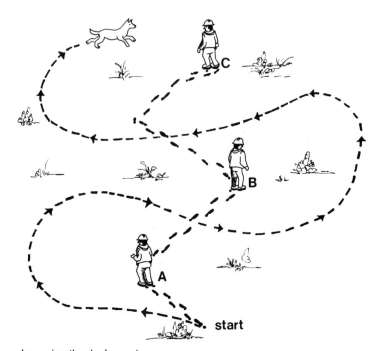

Improving the dog's ranging:
Step 1: As the dog races out ahead, the handler should veer back in the opposite direction.

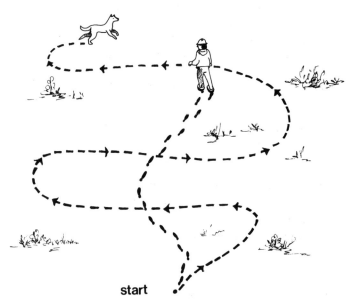

Step 2: As the dog's ranging improves, handler reduces zig-zag pattern while still providing verbal encouragement.   *Linda Warshaw*

is reprimanded while performing correctly and the handler is in error, the dog will become confused. Unjust reprimands may undo several months of training and impair the dog's confidence.

Dogs, like people, are fallible. If it is a bad day for either of you, keep it short and end on a successful note.

Schedule

1. Two to three times each session.
2. Two to three times a week.
3. Practice for two to three weeks.

The dog is ready to move to Step 6 when:

1. It alerts consistently and its alerts are easily recognized.
2. It has flawless close-ins.
3. It generally works the correct distance from you.

STEP 6: FINDING AN UNCONSCIOUS VICTIM

This step concentrates on teaching the dog to find an unconscious or unresponsive person. To do so, the dog must have a foolproof method of letting you know someone is there even if you have not noticed the alert. The ARDA does not teach a barking alert, which may be far too alarming to a victim.

Start with a large field problem with favorable wind conditions so that the dog will pick up the scent from 100 feet or more.

Allow the dog to race all the way into the victim's location (it should be doing this naturally now). As it does so, move off diagonally from the victim's location.

When the dog reaches the victim, the victim remains in place and responds with a quiet, engaging "Hi, Gretchen. You found me. Good girl." The victim also gives the dog a friendly pat. The person should show the ball or stick to the dog, but not let it have the object.

The handler allows the dog time to greet the victim and nose around him, then calls the dog back. As the dog returns, the handler says, "Good girl! Did you find him? Where is he? *Show* me!" The dog may start back immediately and should be encouraged.

If the dog is uncertain, start off toward the victim's location with the "find" command. As soon as the dog heads toward the victim, praise and encourage it forward. Hurry after it to reinforce it the whole way.

Start the praise and play immediately when the dog has led you to the victim.

Practice this regularly, but on some occasions it needs to be omitted, particularly when the dog alerts from a short distance. The dog may think you are not too bright standing a few feet away with the victim obviously right there and not understand what you are trying to do.

A dog eagerly leads its handler back to victim on the refind.   *Ray W. Jones*

Variations

Try the problems in an area approximately one-half mile square, where the victim's location is unknown to you.

As the dog gets better, have the victim become progressively less responsive until the dog will indicate a "dead" victim. Alternate the responsive and unresponsive victims. The dog must understand that, no matter what, it must take you back to what it has found, even if it is a pair of unsuspecting lovers.

Do not use a scent article every time. Any human scent should be checked out and praised, even if it is not the correct one (to the dog, *all* human scent should be "correct").

Try other forms of short interruptions, including water breaks or meeting other handlers. Be friendly, but do not allow the dog to play during breaks. As soon as the short break is over, start out again in a businesslike manner. (There are many short interruptions on real missions.)

Try some night problems. This is the real test of your recall/refind. Since you as a handler have such poor night vision, you will have to rely heavily on your dog. Start in open field areas and progress to light brush.

Try victims in different positions: up a tree, walking, standing, sitting, etc. Scent patterns will differ, and without such variations dogs can become oriented only to victims who lie flat on the ground.

Handlers should start working sectors adjacent to another dog and handler. They should encounter each other occasionally so that the dogs get used to working with other dogs and handlers in the vicinity.

Schedule

1. Three to four times each session.
2. Two to three times a week.
3. Practice for three weeks.

The dog will be ready to move to Step 7 when:

1. It will lead you to the victim's location (unknown to you) at least 80 percent of the time.
2. It leads you to the victim 90 percent of the time despite the fact that you have veered off at least once.
3. It can locate a victim at night 80 percent of the time.

STEP 7: TESTING AND POLISHING SEARCH SKILLS

This is your final preparation for a real search mission. By practicing the following variations you constantly test yourself and the dog in all kinds of situations and find how well you are doing.

1. Do almost all problems where the victim's location is unknown to you.
2. Vary the length of the problems and the use of scent articles.
3. Practice very difficult terrain, heavy brush, large boulders, steep slopes. Start with half-hour problems, then work up to problems that last three or more hours.
4. Try trail running (hasty search) problems where the dog will indicate someone hidden off to the side of a road or trail. Some dogs hate to leave a well-beaten path to plow through the brush.
5. Try several varied terrain problems lasting four hours or more (take short breaks). Use two victims for the first and second time. Plan to find one near the beginning and one near the end of that time. If the dog works well after the second problem, use only one victim.
6. Gradually increase the dog's working time by starting with a one-hour problem. Rest the dog for a half hour or so and then work another one-hour problem. Eventually you will have a dog that will work all day.
7. Take another person with you so the dog is not distracted by an entourage (on searches you will frequently have at least one other person with you). Keep them close behind you and downwind.
8. Try problems in extremes of weather:
   a. Heavy drizzle: work grids very close together and find out at what distance the dog can detect victims.
   b. Poor wind: test detection distance.
   c. Heat: travel slowly and find how well the dog is paying attention with its nose even when it looks tired. Keep the dog well watered and give it a chance to stabilize its panting every so often (heavy panting interferes with scenting).
9. Test your judgment of wind and terrain and the dog's ability to move in on faint scents. A polished search dog will recognize and work a faint scent, thereby requiring fewer passes and less time to search a sector. Start with field problems in a good breeze and know the approximate location of the victim. Estimate where you expect the dog to detect the air scent. Start approximately 200 feet further downwind from your estimated detection zone and run close grids back and forth until the dog picks up the scent. Alternate these problems with the exercise that follows until you are quite accurate at gauging wind conditions.
10. Take a well-defined area and try very wide sweeps to see if the dog can pick up the scent. Utilize natural breaks in the terrain and natural wind funnels. This is called a *hasty search*. If you do not succeed, repeat the search in a more systematic pattern.
11. Try to intersect the latter part of the victim's track and have the dog trail the victim approximately 100 to 200 feet to his location (be sure to cue the dog with a scent article). If the dog fails to respond,

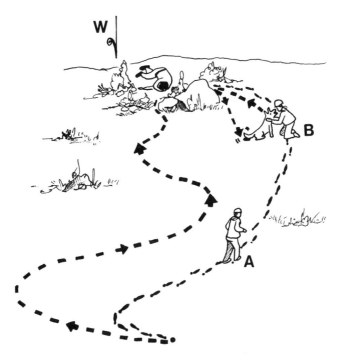

Recall/Refind: At Point A handler encourages dog to close-in on alert; at Point B handler praises dog for returning, then accompanies and encourages it on refind. *Linda Warshaw*

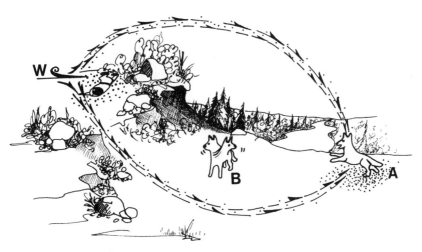

Learning scent diffusion: At Point A dog alerts on scent; at Point B it is in pocket where no scent exists due to diffusion by knoll. Handlers must learn to allow dog to range on either side of obstructions to recover scent. *Linda Warshaw*

do not insist or force it. Complete the problem by going to systematic search sweeps.

12. Leave a jacket or some other article in the search area for the dog to indicate, both as a practice on the indication of clues and to provide a motivational opportunity.
13. Have someone set up several problems for you in strange areas.
14. Work problems that have another dog and handler working an adjacent area.
15. Work problems in areas that have some cows and/or horses. The dog should learn to leave them alone once it has acknowledged their presence.

Much of your training will depend upon how well the dog is doing and whether there is a need to backtrack occasionally to improve on motivation. As you keep your dog in practice for searches, continue to try variations of all the steps.

Reminders

Expect to have a few failures. If you have never had the experience of missing a victim, your training is not complete. Your problems may be too simple or you may be using areas that are too familiar.

It is a good idea—even a practical necessity—to take a two- or three-week break from training. Both the dog and handler can return refreshed and enthusiastic, especially if your training has been regular and consistent.

If your training has been sporadic, it will naturally take longer to reach Step 7. You may find it necessary to cram four to six intensive short working sessions close together to keep the dog from backsliding.

Somewhere along the way you have completed your obedience class. All the obedience lessons should be put to regular use since, at the scene of a search, the dog is in the eyes of the public and must be seen as a well-trained obedience dog. The ARDA has found that dogs with a poor obedience background have limited value as search dogs. They have a definite stopping point and will not work beyond it even though the victim may be close at hand. The obedient dog will go the extra distance because you asked and is usually more successful for that extra effort.

At some point in the latter stages of training, you should accustom your dogs to aircraft (both fixed-wing and helicopter). It is fairly common for the teams to be airlifted to searches. The dogs must learn to on- and off-load aircraft with the engines running to save time and fuel. Handlers must learn safety procedures, how to select landing sites in the event that they must request airlift for evacuation purposes and the weight allowances for the various types of aircraft. This training can frequently be arranged through nearby military bases.

All learning experiences have initial periods of quick learning and re-

Trail problem: X marks location where dog should hit scent in 15 mph breeze if victim is in place at least twenty minutes. *Linda Warshaw*

sponse and then, suddenly, a plateau or even a mild regression. You as a handler may be plunged into despair when your dog suddenly appears to have forgotten half of what it knew or seems to be stuck at some level of training. We call these *learning plateaus*. They inevitably occur between the fourth and sixth week of obedience classes. In search training, you should expect two such plateaus. The first is likely to appear somewhere around Step 5 and constitutes a learning plateau for the dog. The second plateau usually occurs in Step 7 and represents one for the handler.

The first plateau is often solved by reverting back to simple, quick problems with the dog for about two weeks. Sometimes the solution is a two-week break from all training.

The second plateau usually involves the handler being unable to read the dog accurately on longer or more complex problems. This sometimes results from suspecting that the dog is goofing off or thinking that you know better than the dog. In any case, this is a stage that must be worked through (the various parts of Step 7) until you are confident that you know precisely what the dog is doing 95 percent of the time (the remaining 5 percent is confirmed visually).

Schedule

1. One to several exercises each session, depending upon the specific exercises.
2. One to two sessions a week.
3. Utilize all variations for a period of ten weeks.

MAINTAINING YOUR SEARCH DOG

Once your dog has completed the search training outlined in Steps 1–7, you will need to keep those skills polished by practicing the following skill work.

1. Concentrate on special skills like ladder climbing and exercises as described in disaster work.
2. Improve ranging (shorter, frequent problems will produce a ranging dog).
3. Check out old buildings and culverts, etc.
4. Search for objects around and in the house (use the ''look for it'' article-search command).
5. Practice in contaminated suburban areas and around schools or shopping areas (during off hours).
6. Learn elementary avalanche and disaster work techniques even if you do not expect to use them (you never know).

Work the dog on some type of nose problem at least once each week (for example, finding a particular stick with your scent on it in a large woodpile or practicing a short neighborhood search).

A *well-seasoned* dog with two to three years of training can go a month or more without having a good search problem, but it should always have attention and some kind of "nose games." This type of month-long dry spell should be followed by three to four thirty-minute to one-hour problems over a two-week period to keep the dog from becoming rusty. Working regularly is the only way to be sure that the dog is kept in trim.

Hopefully your dog is a house dog that spends 50 percent or more of its time in and around the house or traveling with you. Dogs that are kept kenneled rarely get to spend enough time with their handlers to develop the rapport necessary to travel to strange places and work long hours together. Even when it is not being trained, the dog will be in a learning situation that keeps it alert and interested (for example, behaving when guests are present, learning to play with the cat, not begging at the table, standing still to get brushed). All these incidents teach the dog to recognize subtleties of human moods and normal human commotion and definitely add to its well-rounded personality. The dog is part of your family and has now earned it.

PROBLEM SOLVING

As you progress through various training steps, you may encounter certain problems that indicate you are either progressing too fast or the dog lacks proper motivation. The following are suggestions to help solve some common problems.

1. The dog will not range, working only ten or fifteen feet in front of you in all terrain, including open spaces. This indicates a dog that lacks sufficient motivation and is not really interested in searching. You need to go back to short, easy problems and concentrate on game playing. It may be advisable to stop all search training for at least two weeks and spend that time developing the dog's play drive. When the dog is playing well with you, have other unit members and strangers play with it. Do not start longer problems or use other people as victims until the dog is playing well.

2. The dog is not interested in play with a ball or stick. If you selected a puppy or dog according to the tests recommended in this book, you should not have this problem. It is more likely to occur in older dogs that have never had extensive play sessions.

Your voice inflection will play a critical role, as the dog will pick up on your enthusiasm. You cannot afford to be shy if you want a happy, playful dog. It is usually more successful to start with a ball since its bouncing, rolling action is more likely to attract the dog's interest. Using an excited, happy voice, attract the dog's attention to the ball by holding it in your hand and making short, darting movements with the ball near the ground. When the dog is intently watching, release the ball and let it roll a short distance. If the dog goes after the ball, praise it even if it does not pick the ball up. Try again. If the dog picks the ball up, praise it lavishly. Try one more time, then *quit*. You do not want to bore the dog just as it is showing some interest.

Some dogs respond better to catching a ball thrown to them or chasing one that has been bounced high in the air. Try several different approaches. Repeat this until the dog starts to show real enthusiasm, then gradually increase the distance the ball rolls. If you work, the best play time is immediately after you get home when the dog is excited at seeing you. Use that excitement to your advantage.

If the dog shows no interest in a ball, try a stick or something the dog likes to chew on that is stick-shaped or a knotted old sock and follow the same steps as for the ball. Some dogs may prefer tug-of-war or pursuit, with you chasing it to "get the toy." Either is acceptable so long as the dog enjoys it. As with the ball, stop while the dog is having fun. Even a few brief moments of play are an accomplishment to be built upon.

Experiment. Find whatever turns your dog on. It is *not* recommended that you use a glove, however. You will be wearing gloves in cold weather and on disaster missions and you do not want the dog biting at your hand trying to grab the glove.

If necessary, go to an obedience class or trainer where the dog can be taught to retrieve. Such training should *not* be forced since you want an avid, happy retriever.

A word of caution on ball play and obedience classes: Some obedience instructors use a rolling ball as one test of the sit or down stay. If you are trying to turn your dog into a compulsive player, the last thing you want is to correct it for going after the ball. Politely ask to be excused from this exercise.

3. The dog does not take off enthusiastically on the "find" command, even though it plays with a stick or ball when it finds the victim. This often results when a dog has not yet made the connection between the words *go find* and the act of searching. It is usually seen at the transition from simple problems with visual cues to those where the dog is asked to look for a person who hid before it was brought to the work area.

During the early problems the dog's attention is on the person running rather than on what the handler is saying.

The handler should use the dog's name just before releasing to ensure its attention when the "find" command is given: "Danka, find him!" Reinforce this enthusiastically when the dog closes in: "Good dog! *Find* him!" If necessary, go back to a few runaway-type problems to increase the dog's excitement and to insure it learns the "find" command.

7

Handler Standards and Equipment

IF YOU WERE TO COMPARE search and rescue to painting a picture, the dog would be the brush and the handler the artist: one is a tool and the other directs its action. Without the skilled control of a trained artist, the brush is just an inanimate piece of wood. Likewise, without the direction of a skilled handler, a dog is only out for a walk in the woods.

STANDARDS

No one should contemplate entering search and rescue without realizing that they face months of hard training. A sloppy, half-trained handler is detrimental to the dog, the unit and the entire search and rescue community. The ARDA tolerates no compromise of the standards developed by years of experience. The handler who "doesn't need" to learn first aid or to become self-sufficient in the wilderness has no place in an ARDA unit.

Handlers need to develop a keen sense of the outdoors. The ability to notice and recognize landmarks is very important. They must pay close attention to vegetation, weather and wind conditions and know all will affect the performance of both themselves and their dogs. Above all, they will have to know their dogs' reactions intimately and be able to interpret the dog to the finest degree. This is accomplished through practice and more practice. The handler and dog only become a team when this high degree of performance is reached.

Physical and mental competence and integrity are absolute necessities. It is not unusual for a dog/handler team to be responsible for covering a sector one mile wide by two miles long, regardless of terrain. The ability to go without sleep and still cover the terrain is often necessary. Handlers will have to work at night in complete darkness with only a headlamp, bearing in mind that they may be looking for a body. The later the time, the more unnerving it can be.

Each handler must have a positive attitude. "I will find the person" should always be in the handler's mind. A negative attitude communicates itself to the dog. No one can be absolutely sure where the lost person is, thus each area must be searched thoroughly and conscientiously.

This chapter sets forth the ARDA's handler standards, based on the philosophy that the handler's action should not jeopardize the life of a victim or the effectiveness of the mission.

Stringent standards were developed to ensure that each handler had sufficient training in a multitude of skills. Some of these are used on every mission; some may never be used. All must be learned to prepare the handler for any emergency.

First Aid

Since it only takes a fraction of a second for a *search* to become a *rescue*, no one in search work would consider undertaking missions without first undergoing extensive first-aid training. The ARDA standards specifically require handlers to have Red Cross advanced first-aid training or equivalent. Many ARDA handlers are emergency medical technicians (EMT). Although this level of training is not required for everyone, each unit should have at least one EMT. Cardiopulmonary resuscitation (CPR) training is also highly recommended. Most important, a handler must be certified by the American Red Cross or the appropriate state agency. This not only guarantees a high level of training, but also supplies some protection in the event of a lawsuit.

On many missions, rescue squad personnel are standing by at the base camp, but it may take them an hour to reach the victim's location. The victim may not be able to wait that long for competent medical attention. *You* must be prepared to stabilize the patient and perhaps even help in the evacuation. First-aid courses teach basic transport of a patient to minimize further injury. Expect transport to be even more difficult in the woods. You may have a Stokes litter, but no backboard. You must know how to move an injured person from the ground into a Stokes and then transport without compounding any injuries. You must be able to organize and direct an evacuation, know how to select the safest yet quickest route out of the woods, be prepared to cut a path with a machete and know the correct way to carry a litter over uneven ground without causing undue discomfort to the patient. All this will require training and practice beyond the scope of most first-aid courses.

ARDA units must be able to conduct a nontechnical medical evacuation in wilderness areas.
Bill Syrotuck

The importance of first-aid training is shown as ARDA handler administers to an elderly man found by ARDA dogs.
Emil Pelcak

When taking a first-aid class, pay close attention to the type of injuries common sense would tell you are likely to occur in the woods: snakebite, allergic reaction to stings, broken limbs, burns (from campfires or stoves), cuts, abrasions, gunshot wounds (accidental or suicidal), heart attacks, strokes, diabetic reactions, etc. People who are lost often suffer from medical problems, such as Alzheimer's, which may affect their actions in the woods. In relatively young, healthy people—particularly hunters and hikers—injury must always be considered a possibility. Falls are common, such as slipping off a cliff and landing on a ledge, and you must know how to treat victims who may have suffered a broken back or neck. The wrong treatment could paralyze or even kill them.

The most frequent hazards are *shock* and *hypothermia*. Treat them immediately with all the warmth (inside and outside), rest and reassurance you can. More people die from these two conditions than any injury.

You can be prepared for only a few emergencies. Anything disastrous will usually require more equipment than you can carry in your daypack and a great deal of improvisation. However, skilled first aiders can handle a wide variety of emergencies with the relatively limited supplies they have with them. The equipment you should carry in the field includes:

- Sterile dressing: large, heavy compress with ties (try to get one in a can or waterproof wrap).
- Band-Aids (four to six): good sticky ones for minor personal injuries; when pulled snugly across a laceration or gash it will usually stop bleeding as well.
- Elastic bandage, three inches wide: serves a variety of purposes, from holding a dressing to splinting.
- Aspirin (twelve): a generally safe medication with moderate pain relief (mostly for personal use).
- Safety pins (two to four): serves a variety of purposes.
- Metal mirror: Its clear surface is used to check for moisture to see if a victim is breathing; also used for signaling.
- "Space blanket": used to cover shock or hypothermic victim to help retain body heat.
- Bouillon cubes or instant soup (in paper packet): provides hot liquids to help warm a *conscious* hypothermic victim. Always carry either a metal cup or metal canteen so it can be used to heat the water.
- Snakebite and allergy kits, as needed.

Be sure to keep all items clean and neat in plastic wrappers.

You are accepting an incredible responsibility when you volunteer to look for someone in trouble. You must be prepared to handle it.

Map and Compass

The dog, the radio, the map and compass: any one without the other two will render you virtually useless. The dog is your reason for being there; the radio is your link to the outside world; the map and compass determine the accuracy and ultimate success of your effort.

The topographical ("topo") map serves multiple purposes. It determines your primary search area (when combined with information on the missing person) and sector breakdowns based on existing or arbitrary boundaries. It records the progress of the search based on areas covered and provides planning data for expanded coverage. You cannot conduct a professional, accurate search without a topo map (use of a 7.5 minute or 1:24,000 map is recommended because it details such things as power lines, dirt roads, trails, marshes, etc.).

The ARDA requires an "intimate knowledge" and means just that. Every member of your unit must become extremely proficient with both the map and compass, including base camp personnel. The ARDA recommends the use of Kjellstrom's *Be Expert with Map and Compass* (American Orienteering Service, 1967) as a textbook. Other sources of instruction include local orienteering clubs, a nearby national park that may offer orienteering courses and past or present members of the military.

Orienteering courses will teach the basics of compass use. Competitions in orienteering are based on point-to-point compass work over a prescribed course and against time. Various markers are set along the course that must be reached in a specific order. Although your compass work on a search may not be as precise as the orienteering course, the training is a must. You will be able to do precise work if it is ever necessary (for example, you may be asked to check an old house site in the middle of the woods and must go directly there from base camp).

On searches, your compass work will be much more general. You will set your compass bearing (direction of travel) along one of your boundaries, based upon wind conditions and your search plan, then follow that general bearing to your next boundary rather than to a particular marker. If you work your initial boundary correctly and assess the wind well, your dog's nose will cover the area you do not physically walk through. When you reach your far boundary, you will turn and follow it for whatever distance you think will ensure the dog's detection of anyone between your sweeps. Your passes may be less than 100 feet if there is no wind or up to 300 feet apart if there is a good breeze; vegetation will also determine the width of your sweeps. Once you have made your decision, you will turn and work parallel to your original path, using your compass to direct you. Again, you will be working to a boundary rather than a specific point. Even though you will be working boundary-to-boundary rather than point-to-point, an orienteering course will give you a firm foundation in the use of the map and compass.

On those searches where no topo map is available, handlers will have to rely solely on their compasses and be prepared to draw a detailed map of their area when they return to base. To prepare for this, they must learn to note and remember major terrain features and their path through the sector. This takes a great deal of practice and a real familiarity with map drawing. The best way

Every unit member must become extremely proficient with a map and compass.

Peggy Williams

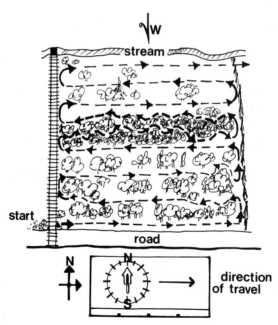

Use your compass "bearing" (direction of travel) to go from boundary to boundary, varying sweep widths to accommodate changes in terrain or vegetation. *Linda Warshaw*

to achieve this skill is to have handlers draw maps of their training problems, even if they had topo maps. They should also practice tracing or drawing their sector from the base map for those instances on a real search when an individual copy for each handler is not available.

Handlers should practice with no map, using only their compasses, and also with no compass, utilizing only terrain features as a guide. Night searching must be practiced because the loss of long-range visibility forces greater reliance on the compass. An excellent training exercise is a night orienteering course; the handler who can work such a precision course at night will have no trouble with a night search. Working a strange woods at night is a real test of a handler's skill and night searches are as common as daylight searches. Failure to do night searching because handlers lack skill in map and compass work is a failure to do the best job for the victim.

Likewise, grid-line search techniques, where handlers only feel secure if others are within a few hundred feet on either side of them, reflect a unit that is not using its teams to their best advantage. This method greatly reduces the working scope of each dog, defeats the purpose of a search dog unit (to cover large areas rapidly and effectively with minimum manpower) and creates unnecessary interference from nearby dogs and handlers.

Units should not begin taking searches until all handlers are capable of working independently, day or night, in any terrain. The role of the map and compass is too critical to approach from a haphazard attitude and handler training in this aspect must be thorough.

Base camp operators must also learn their responsibilities relevant to the use of the map and compass. Base should have some type of map table or board and a clear plastic overlay upon which a felt-tip marker can be used for notations. The base operator will need to mark the following on the overlay:

- The victim's point last seen.
- Each sector boundary and unit number of the assigned handler.
- Any changes to information on the map (new logging roads, etc.).
- Any alerts or clues reported by handlers.
- Areas covered by other resources.
- The base camp location.
- The exact route of the handlers through their sectors.

All of these can be practiced as handlers train in sector searching and during mock searches.

Survival

The ARDA's philosophy on survival expects the handlers to be able to support themselves, their dogs and the victim for up to twenty-four hours if evacuation is delayed due to weather, darkness or terrain. The equipment required must be lightweight yet dependable.

You must be prepared to build a fire, build a shelter and provide food and drink for yourself, your dog and the victim. First-aid equipment must also be carried, as noted previously.

Survival equipment includes:

- Knife: a heavy-duty, Swiss-Army type with multiple blades and accessories is ideal. You may have to cut heavy branches for shelter, for firewood or to make a splint.
- Matches (waterproof and windproof): must be carried in a waterproof container; do not use for lighting cigarettes.
- Rope (about fifty feet, ⅛″ nylon): may be used to help dog down a cliff, to tie a tarp to branches for shelter, for shoe laces, etc.
- Wire or folding saw: used to cut firewood, splints, stretcher poles, etc.
- Whistle (low pitch and loud): supplies directional help to bring evacuation assistance or in case your radio fails.
- Water purification tablets or kit: used to purify water from a questionable water source.
- Canteen: should be metal or have a metal cup so it can be used to heat water. Refill with fresh water each day before leaving base camp and top off at every opportunity.
- Firestarter: commercial items available for starting fires when kindling is damp.
- Plastic tarp (9′ x 12′): supplies shelter.
- Flares (day and night): used for signaling helicopters, base camp, victim location, etc; must be used with extreme caution due to fire danger.
- Food: enough for you, your dog and the victim. This should include at least one emergency meal (freeze-dried), instant soups, high-energy snacks and patties for the dog.

The unit should seek instruction in and then practice the use of improvised gear for overnight survival. They should also be taught about any edible foods available in the woods. Each member should practice setting up a survival camp during a unit overnight training session.

EQUIPMENT

First-aid and survival equipment have already been covered. In addition, there are many other items of personal gear each member must have. Rather than rushing out and buying everything at once, members should gradually purchase these items as their training progresses and they determine what will best suit their needs.

Both handlers and base personnel must be prepared to survive in any climate. ARDA handlers are shown here with backpacks containing gear necessary to support themselves, their dogs and the victim.   *Jeff Doran*

91

Radio

The radio is a critical lifeline between the handlers, base camp and any needed additional medical or agency assistance. It is absolutely necessary that all teams have radios when they participate in real searches. Since a radio can be an expensive item, it is advisable to make this one of the first unit purchases. The unit as a whole should discuss radio communications and the feasibility of different types.

Citizens' Band (CB). CB units are popular and fairly inexpensive. The main advantage is cost. The main disadvantages are the crowded channels, the number of people who will overhear your conversations and the range.

Business and Public Safety Band (FM). These units are more expensive, but have advantages of range, power supply, frequency assignment and a smaller, more flexible antenna. They require special licensing and are used by police, fire and rescue squad personnel.

Amateur Radio. This could be a consideration, although the equipment is relatively expensive and each member would need a license.

A communications officer should be appointed to investigate the various radio systems and required licensing. This person will also be responsible for radio maintenance and communications training within the unit.

Unit codes should be developed to ensure the privacy of communications. Codes should include:

- A number for each unit member.
- The condition of the subject (alive and well, alive but ill/injured or deceased).
- Finding of clues.
- Handler operations (beginning and ending sectors, status check).

A code should also be developed so that the base camp operator can warn handlers to stifle any transmissions if an unauthorized person is near the radio.

Radio communications should be practiced at each unit workout. If you are to be regarded as professional, you must act and *sound* professional. Each member must be well versed on radio procedures under Federal Communications Commission rules and regulations, while base operators are expected to exhibit an above-average knowledge.

All members must have training in basic field trouble-shooting. This will include changing batteries and either repairing or rigging an antenna. Each handler must be prepared to use a click code in case their radio will transmit sounds but not voices. Base camp, upon realizing such a problem, should initiate a series of questions that can be answered by clicks signifying "yes" and "no." The radio is too important to lose because of a minor problem that handlers should have been prepared to overcome.

Handlers must learn to carry the radio safely through the woods, where limbs and briers can easily snap a metal antenna or the "squelch" control can be accidentally turned so base communications cannot be heard.

Radio conversations also interrupt the concentration of the dog and handler. Both must learn to continue as though no interruption ever occurred. As soon as a unit has both the base and hand-held radios, you must begin practice so that radio communication will become second nature.

Clothing and Field Gear

The unit should decide upon a uniform that every member will wear on a search. The uniform makes a group look professional and also makes each member easily identifiable to the agency.

Shirt. The shirt should have long sleeves that can be rolled up during the hot hours of the day and down when working the cooler evening hours. Cotton should be worn during the warm months and wool during cold weather.

Trousers. Trousers should be long (for protection), snagproof, wind resistant and loose fitting (for easy movement and good circulation). Hunters' ''brush'' or ''bush'' pants are useful because of the nylon front that enables briers to slide over them. However, they can be hot in summer and in the winter extra pants should be worn under them.

Jacket. The best jacket is usually some type of mountain parka that is water resistant, snagproof and windproof. It should be a high-visibility color, such as international orange.

Boots. Boots must be heavy duty, lightweight, with a nonslip sole. Use waterproof leather; plain or simulated rubber is dangerous in cold weather or snow. Snow packs are ideal for winter or wet and cold conditions.

Hat. A hardhat is required in the woods for safety purposes, and when flying on military aircraft (a chin strap is also required).

Rain Gear. Suitable rain gear includes durable pants and jackets, which should be a high-visibility color and fit over other clothing. Ponchos do not work well, as they leak and snag easily.

Besides the uniform, members should have the following clothing and field gear.

Underjacket. Most units use these under the parka, which is rarely heavy enough for warmth. Experienced outdoorsmen know the best protection against cold and hypothermia is layered clothing, so layers can be removed or added, depending upon the change in outside temperature.

Gloves. Good leather gloves are required for protection; they are particularly necessary for disaster missions.

Socks. Socks should be made of light wool, or cotton with a second pair of heavy wool.

Personal Pack. This will be left at base. The pack should include: extra socks; a wool sweater; extra shirts and pants; undergarments; lightweight shoes; personal hygiene items; a good-quality sleeping bag, rated to at least $-20°$ F, with pad; stove/fuel/personal eating utensils; and a two-man tent (for you and your dog).

Handler with radio and day pack. *Bill Syrotuck*

An ARDA evaluator checks off equipment as a unit member goes through his field pack.
Penny Sullivan

Personal Field Pack. This should be a fanny pack or similar, for use in the field. This will carry the previously listed first-aid and survival supplies, as well as a headlamp with batteries; spare compass (liquid-filled); adhesive tape; insect repellent; paper and pencil; disposable towelettes; aluminum foil; toilet paper; surveyor's flagging tape; heat packs; extra flashlight bulbs and batteries; and a camera and extra film.

Specific conditions in your region may dictate additions to or deletions from this list. However, each person must carry sufficient equipment to handle any emergency that is likely to be encountered. All the items for the personal field pack can easily fit into a well-made beltbag or fanny pack. Hours of working in rough terrain and weather require a handler to carry as much as possible with as little weight as possible. Each item listed has been selected because it meets this requirement.

All this gear must be readily packed into a flyaway or duffel bag in the event the unit is airlifted to a search. Aircraft are limited in the weight they can carry, so members must know the combined weight of themselves, their dogs and their gear.

The well-equipped, well-trained handler requires months of hard work and no small amount of personal expense. Once you have begun taking searches, however, you will appreciate all the extra time and effort you put into forming a group that can handle any task required.

A central coordinating number enables agencies to contact the ARDA through the River Vale, New Jersey, Police Department.

Detective Timothy Sullivan, River Vale, New Jersey, Police Department

8

The Search Dog Unit

ONCE YOUR UNIT has decided to go ''active'' and made a commitment to the local area to engage in search and rescue activities, it *must* stand behind its commitment. Therefore, it is necessary that the unit be fully trained and equipped to meet its responsibilities at all times.

UNIT ORGANIZATION

If a search situation arises, the unit must respond. Answers such as ''It's too late,'' ''It's too cold,'' ''It's too far away,'' ''We don't have any dogs available'' or ''No one wants to go'' cannot be tolerated. The only answer to a request for assistance is, ''Where do we meet and at what time?''

The unit must be prepared to respond to an average of three calls, with the possibility of ten to fifteen, a month. At least one operational leader (OL) and three other members should be prepared to leave their homes or places of employment within one hour of a call.

The unit must always have an air of professionalism. Members should know exactly what to do and do it with confidence. The dogs will catch the eye of the public and the news media. It is therefore imperative that all dogs behave in a manner that reflects a high degree of training.

In short, if the unit cannot fulfill the responsibility of an active search organization, it should not become active.

Preliminary Structure

The preliminary structure should consist of people who have a strong interest in forming a search unit and have had some dog training experience. They should also have a sound outdoor and camping background.

It is important that the unit be thoroughly trained before it engages in actual search missions, thus the work done in the preliminary phase will certainly determine the group's final outcome. The confidence of responsible agencies will have to be earned by the competence and professionalism displayed by the unit.

Two leadership structures are necessary within a unit, one for administration of the organization and one for search operations. (In small units, these jobs may be combined.) The organizational leadership should include elected officers (president, vice president, secretary and treasurer), who will be responsible for the day-to-day management of the unit's business.

For search operations, an operational leader should be elected from the group with a three-fourths majority of votes to ensure the respect and cooperation of all members. This individual should determine the availability of search management courses, and participate in one or more, as this is a complex skill that requires specialized training.

The unit's success or failure will rest on the shoulders of its leaders, as will the responsibility to see that each of the topics discussed here are carried out. Of course, some responsibilities should be delegated to other members, but the leaders should be fully versed on each subject.

The group has the responsibility of cooperating with the leaders. They should be prepared to spend a considerable amount of time training their dogs and themselves. The unit depends upon teamwork. Failure of one person on the team will reflect upon the whole unit and possibly influence the unit's final outcome. For example, a search area may be reported "clear." If, at a later date, the lost person is located dead within that so-called "cleared" area by other means, one can rest assured that the dog group will never be asked to that jurisdiction again. Not only does this reflect on the group, but also on the value of dogs in search work. With such an incident, the entire philosophy is degraded.

Once it is established that the group meets the requirements, it should proceed in each of the areas outlined in this chapter. The group should not rely on the availability of two or three dogs. The ideal number to start with should be at least six or more highly trained dogs and handlers. The hazard of relying upon only a few dogs is that one may become injured or unavailable and the one or two remaining dogs may be unable to respond to the search that day. Absence of just one dog in this case would leave the unit's efficiency at a low state. A second consideration is handling two or more searches at one time.

On the basis of the information in this chapter, the unit should engage in training for at least one year. One of the greatest hazards in search work is that of a unit committing itself prematurely.

Preliminary Research

A prospective unit should make a careful survey of their area relative to the types of search situations in which they would render aid. The following topics must all be considered.

Subject. Various types of individuals may be involved:

- Aged: senior citizens who have become disoriented in wooded areas.
- Adults: hikers, hunters, etc., who have become lost or injured and have not returned at a predetermined time.
- Teenagers: they may have become lost due to a variety of reasons.
- Children: small children who have wandered away from campgrounds or homes adjacent to wooded areas.
- Evasives: mental patients who hide because they do not want to be found; children who hide because of the fear of punishment; suicide victims who have indicated their intention but have not yet committed the act—many go into wooded areas to commit suicide and do not want to be found.

The subjects outlined present different types of behavior and should be tabulated so that the unit can anticipate the appropriate areas of search and the response of the individual. Obviously, an evasive who is running away behaves quite differently than a hunter who runs toward you for the joy of being found.

Terrain. The types of terrain should be considered and tabulated, as this becomes relative to the ability of the dog and handler as well as the subject: mountainous (below tree line), marshland (wooded plus watered areas), heavily wooded (trees very close together), forested (wooded and open areas). Subjects will take different courses of action relative to the terrain. In mountainous areas hunters tend to follow drainages. Evasives tend to cross marsh areas to evade tracking dogs.

Climate. The climate is very important in determining the dog's ability to scent: sunshine (hot days), rain (downpours or showers), snow (heavy or light), cold (below 0° F); hot (above 90° F); humid (coastal regions); dry (desert areas). A unit in one area of the country may approach a search problem quite differently than another, even though both may be looking for a lost hunter.

Condition of the Victim. The victim may be found in less-than-optimal condition:

- Exposure (hypothermia): subject has inadequate protection against the elements.
- Broken bones: subject has fallen over a cliff or broken an ankle.
- Shock: can be caused by a variety of reasons.
- Unconsciousness: can be caused by a variety of reasons.
- Dead.

Time of Year. Since some dogs may refuse to work under certain adverse conditions, they must be conditioned to work in any of the four seasons: winter (rain or snow), spring (a change in vegetation), summer (climate relative to area), fall (rain, a change in vegetation).

Time of Day. Both dogs and handlers must work during any part of the day or night. Handlers should be aware of the different wind conditions and climate variations that may occur in the same area but change between morning and night.

Area. Different parts of the state will have higher loss rates. Wooded areas draw the hunters, while mountainous areas draw the hikers. These areas should be well plotted.

The importance of research is the ability to simulate. Information for the research can be gathered from sheriff departments' or state agencies' records (such as those in the Department of Emergency Services), newspapers or records of other units. The research should go back at least three years and the information tabulated in such a manner that it can become meaningful. The final data should show what the unit must be prepared for and practice during workouts. Obviously, there are many different combinations, but with good statistics a unit is better able to predict and handle any particular situation.

With the statistics, a unit can practice the most common occurrences. They can reconstruct the situation and try different types of solutions.

In general, the unit should concentrate its training on:

1. Day and night practices.
2. Rain, snow and sunshine practice times.
3. Changes in terrain.
4. Lengthening practice times (dogs should eventually work eight to twelve hours).

Research will dictate the type of training the unit should undergo for both dogs and handlers. If the unit tries to simulate actual conditions by having a mock search from time to time, it will not be caught in a situation completely foreign to it.

Discipline

Along with the cooperation of all members, there is also the requirement for discipline. Both are necessary in training and especially in the field on actual searches.

If a practice session is called for every second weekend throughout the year, members should try to make all of them. This would only constitute twenty-five sessions, but takes a considerable amount of time. In a sense, this effort is considered self-discipline.

Group discipline is also necessary. Once the basic policies have been decided upon, all members must adhere to them. Through discipline the group establishes unity. Occasionally individuals have their own ideas and tend to exercise them. Glory hunters have deliberately left their own area and crossed into another, convinced the victim was there. The hazard, of course, is that if the victim is not found by the glory hunter, he has not only left his assigned area unsearched, but has compromised the area of another handler. It is absolutely necessary for members to follow the policies of the unit and the assignments of the OL. This discipline must be practiced during the training phase.

A saying used by responsible agencies is: "If a member commits an error through ignorance, this indicates poor training; if the error is committed knowingly, this indicates poor discipline." Responsible agencies do not deal with all members, but with the OL, who is ultimately responsible for the unit's performance and therefore will have the final reprimand. It should be known by all members that errors committed will reflect upon the group leadership and upon the unit as a whole.

It is suggested that regular meetings be held along with training sessions to give all members an opportunity to air their ideas. Leaders should be willing to consider and discuss new ideas. Once the idea has been accepted or rejected, the group must follow the final decision.

Operational leaders should always be prepared for the worst possible search mission in their area. They should also maintain the unit in a state of readiness for this type of situation so that when it does occur, the unit's performance will reflect the high standard of excellence the group has tried so hard to attain.

Deportment

Discipline ensures that an order will be carried out, but deportment concerns *how* it is carried out. It is important for the group to achieve and maintain a professional attitude and appearance.

All members should wear appropriate clothing: good boots with Vibram soles, and a unit uniform that looks and is appropriate for the task at hand.

All members should know their functions to avoid confusion, misunderstandings or arguments. If an OL makes a request, the member should carry it out quietly and efficiently. Disagreements should be aired later and privately.

Everyone should look as though they have a job and be busy, whether preparing their own gear or helping someone else. Avoid standing around and talking; searches and training sessions are not social encounters.

Avoid panic situations. Through good training, members should not panic. A group's first successful find can be a memorable event; do not turn it into a catastrophe. Occasions have occurred where, in excitement, members could not remember the radio call sign, their voices were higher than normal, their speech garbled and the entire context meaningless.

Only operational leaders should confer with the search director. Avoid situations where the whole group descends upon the director to voice their

Handlers must learn to work together to ensure the search is well-coordinated and all areas covered.   *Jean Syrotuck Whittle*

A unit coordinator takes down information on an incoming search call.
Penny Sullivan

opinions on how the problem should be solved. Neither OLs nor members should ever imply that a search is being mishandled.

Avoid making demands of responsible agencies or leaders. If the group has not been called early enough, try the best you can anyway.

Avoid making excuses. In training sessions, if the dog is not working or the handler has committed an error, accept it and learn from it. You cannot make excuses on a real search—someone's life may be at stake.

The ability to get long with others should be one of the basic criteria. The system requires teamwork and any one person may so antagonize the other members that, instead of working toward unity, they become separated through anger. The handlers will be experiencing many hardships and the OL will be pushing teams to the limit, thus it takes very little to produce unrest unless all are pulling together.

DEVELOPING A UNIT COORDINATING SYSTEM

Once the unit has reached a state of proficiency where it feels ready to take on real missions, it must develop a coordinating system whereby handlers can be notified quickly of an impending mission. This is especially true in avalanche and disaster work. There are several methods by which this can be accomplished.

One coordinator can be established to receive the incoming call from the agency and, in turn, quickly notify the handlers of the mission. This coordinator should have access to the telephone as close to 100 percent of the time as possible. If you contact your nearest Handicapped Association, you may find a handicapped person who is bedridden or handicapped in such a way that he or she is restricted to home nearly all the time. These individuals have fulfilled this role perfectly.

Having a single telephone number for agencies to call eases their job to get in touch with you and is more efficient for the team. The role of the coordinator is to receive the incoming call, get an elementary description of the type of mission and record the caller's name and phone number. The coordinator will then contact the unit's operational leader and take instructions on who to call, along with any specific instructions as necessary.

If there is no single coordinator, the unit can provide a list of numbers to the agency. The agency will then call each number in sequence if there is no answer at the first number. Units will establish a duty roster ensuring that one of the numbers is manned at all times. The procedure from that point becomes the same as in the first example once contact with the unit member has been made. This system is less desirable, as agencies often have to spend time going through four or five numbers. Not only does this waste time, it is also frustrating if time is of the essence.

Another coordinating system also involves the use of a single telephone number. However, once contact has been made the duties are subdivided to other designated persons. The first coordinator will inform two other subcoordinators, who each have specified numbers to call. Consequently, two coordinators will be working at the same time. This system is twice as fast as the others, but the need for such a system will depend upon the size of the unit. In a unit with twenty to thirty members, all can be contacted quickly in this manner. If there are only ten members, a single coordinator may suffice.

For the very brief intervals when telephones are unmanned, an answering machine can be attached to the phone. It can inform the caller of the next number to call or record a message. Call-forwarding can be used to automatically forward calls to a manned number.

Coordinating systems are needed to facilitate rapid notification of handlers. The more efficient the system, the more efficient the unit.

COORDINATING A MISSION

On receipt of a call, the coordinator should secure the following information:

1. Subject category (elderly, hunter, etc.).
2. Length of time the search has already been in progress.
3. Weather conditions under which the handlers will be working.
4. Type of terrain to be searched and if a topographical map of the area is available.
5. Any special considerations.

Items 1 and 2 are straightforward, 3 is important to a centrally based unit. Knowing something about the environment will help in selecting the proper clothing and equipment. During rain and damp weather, the handlers are advised against using down clothes. Snow and higher altitudes call for good wool or down clothing, snowshoes or skis and adequate changes of clothing. Searching in very hot weather calls for an entirely different ensemble of cotton and light wool. It is vital that the coordinator find out what the unit is getting into.

Knowing something about the terrain will help in determining which type of equipment to have on hand. Ice axes, snowshoes and crampons should be used by handlers working snow slopes, glaciers and, in some cases, rocky terrain. All units should consider maintaining some of this snow gear since approximately 75 percent of the country receives significant snowfall.

Environments and terrain can go from one extreme to the other when one considers that search and rescue missions occur throughout the United States. Units will have to define what portion of that spectrum they wish to work in. They may decide to take any and all types. If so, they will have to be prepared for the rigors of Mount McKinley in winter and Death Valley in the summer. To take on the whole spectrum, handlers will have to possess a wardrobe to combat extremes in weather, the equipment to handle the extremes of terrain and the knowledge to survive and work in the extremes of both.

If the unit decides to limit its activities to certain types of missions, it should be aware of other units that can handle the mission beyond the scope of their own unit and be able to make a referral to the agency. Units or handlers should not attempt missions over their heads. However, do not be afraid to try something new or different in your area. Advise the agency of what you estimate the possibilities to be and state that you are willing to try.

Interviewing persons found by the unit can add to research on victim behavior.   *Emil Pelcak*

Units must be prepared to set up base in remote locations where self-sufficiency is required.
Bill Syrotuck

9

Unit Training

THERE ARE two main purposes for unit workouts: to set up problems for each dog, and to exercise the unit in synchronizing a search for one victim. The unit should either alternate each workout to accommodate each purpose or accomplish both at the same workout, depending upon the needs of the unit.

Schedules

Workouts are scheduled one or two times a month throughout the year. Small groups that live near each other can work together between times so long as beginning handlers are thoroughly briefed on training procedures. New units often schedule weekly sessions, particularly until they are "operational." Once operational, they may reduce their training to once or twice a month with handlers working their dogs on motivational problems between unit training sessions.

Each unit must determine what schedule works best to accommodate the members' various levels of training. A person who is skilled at both dog and handler training should be appointed as training officer. It will be this individual's responsibility to schedule all workouts.

Workout Problems

For individual dog problems, the "victim" should be thoroughly briefed on where to be and how to behave (play, lie still, talk, etc.) when found by the dog.

Generally, advanced dog handlers *should not* know where their victim is located. Beginning dog handlers *should* know the general location of their victims most of the time. Intermediate dog handlers may know, depending on the training required.

Good workouts require careful planning, lay out in advance, preparing the area so that there is maximum work time for the dog and minimum time to get the victim(s) in and out of place. Use good boundaries at first.

Have enough victims to go around. Use adults for problems of long duration.

When each dog of the unit has an 80 percent success rate on individual problems, the training officer can start working them simultaneously on sector problems under simulated search conditions. The training officer will place one victim in a large area. That area is divided into sectors and the dogs start searching. This should be practiced frequently, as each dog will have to be aware of the other dog's presence (even if it is a quarter mile away). When first practicing such a search problem, each dog that worked a sector with no victim should be given a short motivational find at the end.

Utilize part of the time to teach base camp procedures and equipment, radio operations, checking on outdoor skills, navigation, evacuation techniques, group obedience and agility practice, and to test field gear and equipment.

Workouts are never canceled due to weather. If roads are dangerous, use another area.

Evaluation Tests

An evaluation committee should be formed under the leadership of the training officer. It will be their responsibility to establish and administer tests that each dog/handler team must pass prior to becoming operational. These tests can be performed during scheduled unit workouts, with a written record kept of each.

The ARDA uses the following evaluation tests: open field, trail (hasty search), light brush, dense brush, night problem and multiple-victim problem. The test areas range from a trail one-half to one mile in length to an area one-quarter square mile (one-half mile long by one-half mile wide) or larger. Tests may last from one hour for the hasty search to six hours for the multiple-victim problem. The tests are designed to observe the eagerness, ranging, recall/refind and long-term working ability of the dog, as well as the handler's ability to use a map and compass, evaluate and physically handle a variety of terrain and read the dog.

PRACTICING SEARCH METHODS

The Sector System

The sector system, developed by SARDA after several years of research, should be the basis for all unit searching. Originally referred to as the "corridor system," the ARDA changed the terminology in the 1970s because so many non-ARDA handlers incorrectly assumed that "corridor" meant that the dogs were to be used on a grid line with each spaced only a few hundred feet apart.

The sector system was developed because a search area is normally quite vast. It may encompass 360° from where a person stands and may extend several miles in any direction. At first glance, the area is overwhelming. The solution, therefore, is to subdivide the area into sectors and to assign a dog to each sector, with all searching simultaneously. The sectors are divided from each other by geographical features, such as ridges, drainages, roads, streams, etc., which define the boundaries. A dog and handler may then be responsible for the area bounded by two ridges and a stream or any other configuration that is easily recognizable.

For example, an area between two streams (approximately one mile apart) and bounded by a peak at the far end and a road at the near end (two miles apart) is assigned to one dog and handler. One mile from the stream that forms one boundary of the first sector is a power line running to the peak. A second sector is defined as the area between the power line and the stream common to the previous sector, the peak and the road. The second sector is assigned to a second dog and handler. Obviously, with six dogs the area can be divided into six sectors or the search area can be expanded with each working equally large areas.

The most important part of sector searching is teamwork. Coordination is the responsibility of the operational leader, and radio communications are essential. The operational leader must know what is happening at all times and know the progress of each team. The teams must know the locations of each other and their progress. Inexperienced teams tend to continually find each other. This is due to several factors:

- Inability of the handlers to stay within their boundaries.
- Inability of the dogs to ignore fellow searchers.
- Handlers not keeping good radio contact and describing progress.
- Handlers not watching their compass.

To ensure accuracy, all the skills required for sector searching must be constantly practiced at unit workouts.

Before handlers can begin working sectors, they must understand how to utilize wind currents, terrain features and their map and compass. One of the best training techniques for new handlers is to accompany experienced handlers several times to observe how they subdivide and work their sectors.

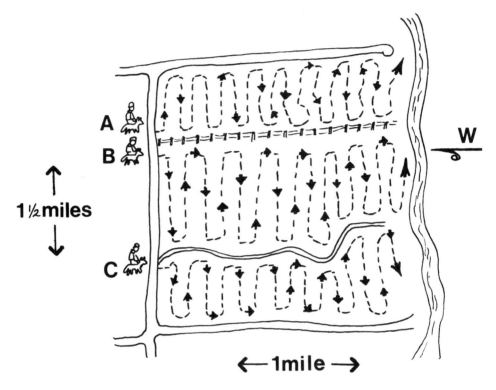

Obvious boundaries (fence, stream and road) should be used to divide sectors.   *Linda Warshaw*

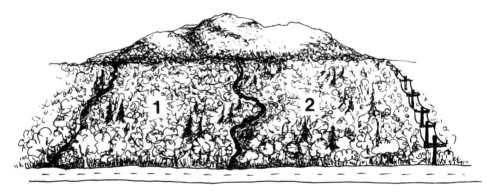

An area between two streams, the peak and road is assigned one handler (1); the area between the stream, power line, the peak and road is assigned to a second (2).   *Linda Warshaw*

Periodically, experienced handlers should in turn accompany trainees to answer questions and provide guidance.

Handlers should develop their search plan before leaving base, including setting the compass bearing they will follow. Once this basic plan is decided upon, only pronounced changes in weather or terrain should alter it. Changing a plan midsector may result in leaving large "holes" in coverage and greatly reducing the probability of detection. However, some sectors contain such a variety of terrain (drainages, small knolls, etc.) that the same pattern cannot be applied throughout. In those cases, it would be advisable to subdivide the sector and work each feature with a different, more appropriate pattern.

When possible, sectors should be approached from a starting point near base. If the wind is coming from the wrong direction, transport should be arranged for the dog/handler teams if they must travel rather long distances to an appropriate starting point. If there is no way to transport the teams, they may be required to walk the distance and then begin their systematic sweeps. This walk often can be utilized to perform a hasty search along a natural or man-made terrain feature.

As they begin working their sectors, handlers will make judgments of sweep widths based on the density of vegetation and wind velocity (that nice breeze in base camp may be nonexistent in the woods). The width of sweeps may vary throughout the sector due to differing levels of vegetation, terrain features and wind speed variability. However, the basic plan devised in base, once begun, must be adhered to regardless of changing conditions. If the handlers feel that the conditions shifted so much as to be detrimental to thorough coverage of certain portions, those portions may need to be rechecked later in the search.

When working their sectors, handlers must pay close attention to numerous details: the dog's body language and working attitude; the map and compass; terrain features, which may or may not be marked on the map; wind direction and velocity; radio traffic; clue and track awareness; and hazards, which may range from cliffs to poisonous snakes. Handlers should not attempt any night work until they have thoroughly mastered these skills during daylight training sessions.

Handler training should include "man tracking" so that they are always clue conscious, even when working at night. A flashlight can often illuminate a track as well as, if not better than, sunlight. As the handlers conduct their hasties or sectors, they should always be alert for any sign that someone has been through the area.

Handlers must always remember that the crux of a good search is a *good plan*. Following the dog on every minor alert is an excellent way to destroy the basic plan and end up with incomplete coverage. Handlers who observe alerts should stop to see how far the dog goes. If it only moves a relatively short distance before losing the scent, it may have encountered either scent residue, perhaps left by previous searchers, or scent drifting in from a dis-

A dense brush problem.   *Jean Syrotuck Whittle*

An open field problem.   *Jean Syrotuck Whittle*

tance. In either case, continuance of the planned search pattern will move the dog closer to any potential scent source. If, on the other hand, the alert is strong and continued so that the dog begins to leave the handler's sight, the handler should also move in that direction, making sure that they can return to the point where the sweep was interrupted. If the alert fails to produce a find, the dog and handler can return to the indicated point and resume their search pattern.

As noted earlier, during training sessions handlers should practice drawing their route on a map as they work the sector. This will help them to learn to observe terrain features and to be "generally aware of their location at all times," as required in the ARDA standards. This skill is critical since it provides the data for the probability of detection and percentage of coverage within each sector on a search. Handlers must be able to tell the operational leader how thoroughly they covered their area ("I will assign an 85 percent coverage of my sector since there was a good, steady breeze and very little dense vegetation") and the probability of detection ("Because of the good wind and terrain conditions, I think there was a 90 percent chance my dog would have found the person").

Not all sectors on the same search can give the same percentages. Dense swamps or woods may have a very low detection and coverage rate and those areas may have to be rechecked. Handlers must avoid the "superdog syndrome." Do not assign high coverage and detection percentages on the assumption it makes your unit look good. Leave a little room in case one dog was not really working to its usual standards or a handler made a mapping error. No unit is ever 100 percent sure, even under the best of conditions.

Upon completion of their sectors, handlers must be prepared to explain why they worked their area in a particular way. There will be some occasions that demand ingenuity or deviation from the usual crosswind pattern. One example is a steep slope. If the wind is moving up- or downslope, it can be worked in the usual way by going back and forth across the slope. If, however, the wind is coming from one side, the handler may elect to still work back and forth on the contours since it is far less tiring than repeatedly climbing up and down. Working into the wind in such cases reduces the detection responsibility since, on half of the sweeps, the wind will be angling from behind the dog/handler team. Either the sweeps can be greatly narrowed to allow more thorough coverage or the search can be treated as a hasty, with the lesser probability of success that implies. Handlers must be prepared to make such adjustments and decisions when planning their search.

The Hasty Search

The hasty search is intended to provide a rapid, though cursory, check of the overall search area. It serves several purposes:

- To assess terrain prior to a more thorough sector search.
- To quickly check areas of high probability, such as drainages or paths that may have "funneled" the victim.
- To provide an immediate search technique if handlers have driven a long distance and/or arrived after dark, when a sector search lasting several hours might be counterproductive.

Hasties can be run along trails and drainages, with the handler making occasional loops into the woods (following game trails branching off an old road provides one effective way to increase coverage). They can also be conducted along power lines or even around old buildings to check quickly for a small child who may be hiding. Sectors assigned for the next day can be given an initial coverage at night by working perimeter boundaries and/or making one or two wide sweeps through the area. It is advisable for handlers to flag trails, etc., with surveyor's ribbon to mark those areas that have been covered.

While hasty searches are frequently conducted at night, one or two handlers may be assigned to perform such a search within minutes of arrival on scene during the day as the balance of the unit prepares for full field deployment.

This technique, as with sectors, must be practiced by handlers because wind conditions are not always perfect. A trail may have to be worked into the wind or eddying may create problems for the dog in following scent to its source. In such cases, it must be remembered that a hasty is exactly what its name implies—a quick search that does not necessarily guarantee success. However, the number of people found by this method has shown it to be highly effective for the amount of time expended.

To prepare for hasty searching, handlers should practice running trails, power lines, etc. The dog should show a willingness to leave the beaten path when it picks up scent; at times, the dog may be required to follow a track where the victim has crossed the path rather than the air scent.

The value of practice in all types of terrain and weather will be proven on actual searches where handlers must make critical assessments of the best approach to their sectors. The unit as a whole should strive for an overall coverage of 85 percent, including both hasties and sectors. To achieve this will require hours of practice in thorough coverage of a large area, with all handlers recognizing the critical role they play in the unit's success.

Radio Communication

During search training, both the handlers and base operators should practice radio communications. After approximately one hour, base camp should begin a systematic radio check with all handlers to determine their location within each sector. Handlers must be prepared to respond with close grid locations and base personnel must mark those locations on the map.

Any communications initiated by the handlers must be concise and pertinent. These communications may include:

The search area may be quite vast.   *Penny Sullivan*

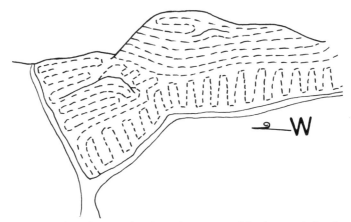

Example of varying search patterns to accommodate changes in terrain and still utilize wind currents.   *Linda Warshaw*

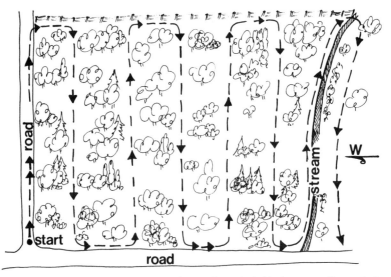

Typical cross-wind sector pattern, starting on downwind side (sweeps will vary, but are normally 100 to 300 feet apart).   *Linda Warshaw*

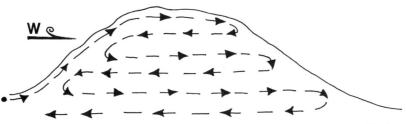

Work a steep slope across rather than up and down.   *Linda Warshaw*

116

- Reporting a clue.
- Requesting to meet another handler for consultation on boundaries.
- Reporting alerts, including those that seem to originate in an adjoining sector (handlers *do not* blindly charge into another handler's sector without first clearing it with the operational leader, base *and* the other handler).
- Reporting an injury or illness of the dog or handler.
- Requesting transport back to base after completion of the sector.
- Finding the missing person.
- In general, the best rule is silence unless you have extremely important information.

Variations of Search Problems

Training sessions should include, at various times, victims who are lying prone, sitting, walking, standing still, up in a tree, buried under leaves and brush, etc. The dogs must learn to find people in a wide variety of positions and situations.

The length of each problem will depend upon the training level of the team. Eventually, an operational dog should be expected to work problems lasting several hours.

One method of extending problems for each dog and at the same time practicing multiple-victim finds (so the dogs will not stop after finding one person since actual searches often result in unexpected finds of people who are not lost) is the *round robin technique*. For example, there may be four victims hidden, one in each of four sectors. Each dog team starts with their assigned sector and, after finding the victim, moves to the next free sector and searches for that victim. Persons willing to play the role of the victim should understand that they may be in the woods for several hours, and they must be prepared to "make themselves at home" (most take along food, drink and even books).

On occasion, articles should be dropped within each sector. This serves several purposes. The dog learns to indicate a clue with human scent, while the handler can practice watching the dog closely for what may be a minor indication (since the article has less scent than the victim). In addition, it provides a motivational opportunity for the handler to play with the dog, particularly if the problem lasts several hours.

Night searching must also be regularly scheduled since it is not at all unusual for units to receive at least half of their calls late enough to require working at night.

ADDITIONAL TRAINING

Classroom instruction should be given in scent theory, survival, map and compass, unit procedures, wilderness evacuation and search management. All these will, of course, be practiced in the field, but the basics should be taught in a classroom atmosphere where questions can be asked and suggestions considered. Experts in other fields, such as veterinarians or disaster heavy rescue specialists, may also be brought in to lecture.

Representatives from other search organizations or official agencies may be invited to either lecture or attend your training sessions. You must learn the search structure within your state—who is in charge of what—and then establish a rapport with those who will request your services long before a search ever occurs. Any unit that fails to do this may not get calls. ARDA units only respond *when requested* by an official agency because to do otherwise appears unprofessional. Should you invite yourself in, an agency may agree to let you come after you call, but you will probably be met with a reluctant welcome. On the other hand, if you respond at *their* request, you will be there because they *want* you and the atmosphere will be much more cooperative. Do your meeting and greeting before an agency actually needs you and leave the decision to them.

BASE CAMP

The unit's base camp is far more than a place to eat and a communications center. It becomes the hub of your search and serves as the operation's eyes and ears while handlers are in the field. Good base camp operators (BCOs) are critical to a unit's success; poor ones can destroy a unit's reputation. As stated earlier, unit workouts should always include practicing some or all aspects of base operations.

All unit members must be sufficiently skilled in running base camp to enable them to substitute or assist when necessary. Handlers whose dogs are temporarily sidelined by illness or injury and trainees whose dogs are not yet operational should be prepared to work in base.

What should BCOs prepare for? Virtually everything. A breakdown of their duties will explain why they must be highly trained in a multitude of skills.

BCO Responsibilities

Radio Communications. Often, the only continuous exposure an agency has to a unit's operation is through observation of the base camp. Agencies follow strict radio procedures and they will expect the same from a volunteer unit. The BCOs should control all the unit's radio traffic. It may be advisable for handlers who wish to communicate with each other to first clear it with base to ensure that they do not interfere with other transmissions they might not be receiving on their own radio. Transmissions must be succinct, as nothing can make a unit appear more amateurish than constant chatter on the radio. The BCOs are responsible for ensuring the unit uses proper radio codes and adheres to all Federal Communications Commission regulations (including appropriate use of a call sign). All transmissions must be maintained on an accurate radio log.

Additionally, the BCOs are responsible for radio security so that unauthorized persons do not overhear transmissions. They must also be prepared to relay pertinent information and/or decisions to the OL. Unit codes must be used since base security does not prevent those with citizen band radio base stations or police scanners from overhearing your conversations.

Map and Compass Skills. The BCOs must be as well trained in this aspect as the handlers. They must be able to describe the sectors and search plan and to define a given handler's location within a sector. They will be responsible for advising evacuation personnel of the handler's location when the victim is found and the best route to that site.

Search Management Training. If the operational leader is temporarily out of contact and the agency has questions about the search plan or seeks suggestions for use of other resources, the BCOs must be prepared to answer. A knowledge of subject behavior, terrain analysis and resource management is required for these situations. The agency may regard your unit as the experts and the BCOs must be prepared to provide such assistance with confidence. It is advisable for the operational leader to leave information on potential future search areas with the BCOs so that they can automatically assign those either to handlers who have finished their first assignment or to other resources.

Public Relations. The one thing BCOs cannot afford is arrogance. Because of their continuous presence, the BCOs most represent the attitude of your entire unit. They must be friendly yet professional and businesslike with the agency, sympathetic and understanding with the subject's family and friends and pleasant without being too talkative to the press. They cannot give the family false hope, nor can they be too discouraging. They can give the media general information about the dog unit (how the dogs and handlers are trained, etc.), but they must refer specific questions about the search to the agency. In short, BCOs must be blessed with diplomacy and tact.

Logistics. The BCOs are responsible for selecting the appropriate campsite based on traffic flow and proximity to the agency's command post. Setting up a full base operation for both local and remote situations must be practiced during unit workouts to prepare for actual missions and to test equipment. All unit personnel must be prepared to help set up the base antenna, tarp, radio, tents and cooking equipment.

The BCOs are also responsible for overseeing the well-being of the unit. They must ensure that food and drink, appropriate to the climate and working conditions, are available and they must make sleeping arrangements, if needed. They must see that sanitation rules are followed and that the base area is cleaned before the unit departs.

First Aid. The BCOs must meet the same standards as the handlers and be prepared to handle emergencies in base camp. They will have to coordinate

Base camp serves as a briefing, communications and dining center for the unit.

Bill Syrotuck

Setting up the typical ARDA base camp.

Tim Sullivan

any medical evacuation, including advising local personnel what extra medical supplies should be taken along. They must be aware of the needs of handlers, both in nutrition and equipment, who will spend hours working under extreme conditions. They must maintain and know how to use both the human and dog first-aid kits maintained in base camp.

The job of base camp operator is one of the most difficult in the unit and frequently requires two people. A unit cannot perform to its professional best without good BCOs.

Recommended Base Equipment

Tenting. A four- or six-man tent can house several dog/handler teams or serve as the communications center.

Food. The base camp must stock at least a five-day supply of freeze-dried meals for handlers; nutritious, high-energy snacks; coffee, tea and cold drinks; as well as a five-day supply of dog food (handlers should provide this to be stored at base since each dog may have different dietary requirements). It must also provide cooking equipment, including stoves, fuel, utensils, plates, cups, garbage bags and collapsible water containers (a water purification system or tablets should be included).

First Aid. An extensive first-aid kit should be maintained at the base. It should include bandages, dressings, cravats, air and/or board splints, antibiotic medications, antivenom and insect sting medications, a low-reading thermometer, scissors, tweezers and, if possible, a Stokes or similar litter for medical evacuations. A separate dog first-aid kit should also be kept in base.

Radios. These include the base radio, base antenna, hand-held units with at least one spare, battery chargers, extra batteries, voltmeters, spare antenna for the hand-held units and a radio repair kit (small tools, screws, nuts, bolts, etc.).

Documents and Miscellaneous Supplies. These should include blank forms (interview sheets, radio logs); pens, pencils, markers; plastic sheeting for maps; tracing, writing and drawing paper; grids, protractors and rulers; paper clips and staples; compasses; clipboard; map board for use by the BCO; a list of emergency/contact numbers for unit personnel; flashlights and batteries; unit brochures/handout sheets (useful to give the agency and the news media). Other equipment may include hatchets, hammers, small shovels, camp lights, etc.

The well-planned, well-organized base camp operation will give your unit an air of professionalism and ensure that your mission runs more smoothly. Do not be so anxious to train dogs that you overlook or shortchange this extremely important facet of search and rescue.

SUMMARY

Unit workouts must accomplish the following:

1. Train advanced dogs in extended working times, working in varied terrain, locating victims in unusual positions or situations, advanced agility and obedience.
2. Train advanced handlers in sector coverage, radio communications, medical evacuation, map and compass work, base operations and night searching.
3. Train base operators in radio communications, maintaining written records, mapping, dealing with personnel on a search and setting up and using base equipment.
4. Train new handlers in dog handling, map and compass, sector coverage, scent theory and unit operations.
5. Train new dogs in searching, agility and obedience.
6. Refine unit procedures to ensure teamwork and thorough coverage.
7. Train unit specialists, such as the operational leader, medical officer and communications officer, through mock searches, simulated medical evacuations, etc.
8. Introduce the unit to outside groups and agencies involved in different aspects of search and rescue.

A typical training session may be as follows:

9:00 A.M. to Noon: Advanced dog/handler teams work sectors and/or undergo evaluation tests. Each dog may find a victim, or the workout may be a mock search with only one victim placed. Trainees can assist by serving as victims or observing the advanced teams work their sectors.

Noon to 1:00 P.M.: Entire unit practices setting up base camp; new members are expected to help so they learn the various duties. Lunch is served using unit cooking equipment.

1:00 to 2:00 P.M.: New handlers work a basic orienteering course.

2:00 to 4:00 P.M.: New dog/handler teams do line-of-sights on handlers, or similar beginner problems. While these should be practiced at home, the training officer must ensure that new teams are proceeding properly. Many new handlers assume that their dog is ready to advance simply because it comes looking for them with such eagerness; the training officer may have to curb their desire to start the dog "looking for someone else" before it is really ready. Development of the dog's play drive, particularly with nonfamily members, should be included as part of this session.

All unit workouts should be followed by a critiquing session to help with individual or unit problems. The training officer should maintain a written record of each session and of the critique itself.

10

Responding on a Search

Y OU NOW FEEL your dog/handler teams are competent and operationally ready. You are prepared to take on actual search missions. Before accepting missions, your coordination system must be well established so that the initial search call is handled smoothly and rapidly.

CALL-OUT AND RESPONSE

During call-out, the operational leader will determine both the number of unit members responding and a commitment time for each (the unit as a whole should plan on an average commitment of three days). The agency can then be advised of how many members will be arriving and how long the dogs will be available.

Once a decision to respond has been made, the rendezvous time and place must be established, assuming all personnel are in a state of readiness to be on their way within one hour of call-out. The rendezvous is necessary to ensure that the unit arrives as a structured, professional organization with members immediately assuming previously assigned tasks. On rare occasions, the OL may instruct one or more *experienced* handlers who live near the search site to proceed ahead of the unit, conduct the initial interviews and perhaps run hasty searches near the "point last seen."

The agency should be given an approximate arrival time based on the driving distance between the rendezvous point and the search site. Since there may be a considerable time lapse from the initial call to arrival at the scene, you should encourage searching with other resources until you arrive. Agencies that do not work frequently with air-scenting dogs may assume that the area must be kept clear because they are often given those instructions when a tracking dog is used. A brief explanation of how the dogs work will help the agency understand why it is not necessary to immediately suspend all other search efforts.

Once the unit arrives at the search, the OL should locate the agency representative to ascertain the current situation and base personnel should select the best location for base camp.

SETTING UP BASE

The agency often already has a command post established and the BCOs must select an appropriate site utilizing what space is available. This site should be in close proximity to the agency's command center for constant liaison, yet should not be in the middle of the main traffic flow. Dozens of people may be wandering through the area and you do not want them lounging around your base, listening to what could be sensitive radio communications and distracting the BCOs.

The BCOs must also consider convenience factors, such as being close to dining and sanitation facilities. Space should be allowed for setting up cooking equipment and a tarp if one is used to provide a covered work or eating area.

When possible, all unit vehicles should be parked together, including the one used as base. Such an arrangement allows for the unit handlers to leave their dogs in their vehicles when required and ensures that all equipment is quickly available.

Remote search locations present an entirely different situation. The agency may have a staging area where vehicles are parked and searchers are shuttled to the command post. Under such circumstances, one unit vehicle may be allowed in the command post area to serve as the unit's headquarters and all unit equipment will have to be transported in it. Even that one vehicle will be eliminated if the unit is flown into the search. For these reasons, the unit must have "flyaway bags" that contain everything it will need to function.

When establishing a remote camp, it must be divided into several areas: a sleeping area, where handler tents are set up; an eating area with cooking equipment and, preferably, some type of lightweight shelter; a base operations center with the base radio and antenna; and sanitation facilities.

Common sense must be used when establishing a remote base. The area used for sanitation must be well away from any water supply. Tents set up in a drainage rather than on a hill could become extremely uncomfortable during

The operational leader is the only member who confers with agency representatives.
Courtesy National Park Service

Base camp operators should ensure food and drink are available to handlers before they enter the field. *Emil Pelcak*

Remote base setup showing separate areas for dining, sleeping, parking and command post operations. *Linda Warshaw*

a heavy rain. Fires must be correctly contained and thoroughly extinguished.

Other unit members assist in base by setting up any external radio antenna, tarp or other equipment and check hand-held radios to ensure that they are in good working order. Drinks and snacks should be prepared and available to handlers prior to their entering the field, as well as ample water for the dogs. Handlers not assisting with base should be getting their gear and dogs ready or helping others in doing so.

While unit members are setting up base and/or preparing their gear, all dogs should remain in the vehicles or be kept on leash. It does not look professional to allow loose dogs to tear around the base camp, and the dogs will use up valuable energy they will need in the field.

Each member must be busy to preclude the unit being rushed into the field by family members anxious to see the teams begin working. Obviously, you cannot allow this to happen until you have all the pertinent information; the sight of people hard at work will help deflect such pressure.

While so working and providing a professional atmosphere, the unit must guard against appearing aloof to other searchers. A friendly attitude, in the midst of your preparation, is often beneficial since information may be offered by people who have already been in the field.

INFORMATION GATHERING

Once initial contact with the agency representative has been made, the OL must obtain as much information as possible and should ask permission for a unit interviewer to talk to family members, friends and/or witnesses. Information gained from these sources is vital, as the unit's search plan will be based to a great extent upon the data developed from these interviews.

Searching Information

During the interview process, certain searching information must be obtained and provided to each handler. The unit should develop an interview form upon which to record all necessary searching data, including:

- Subject's name.
- Physical description (height, weight, race, etc.).
- Clothing description.
- Shoe size and tread.
- Discardables to watch for as clues (cigarette brand, chewing gum or candy wrappers).
- Equipment the subject may have carried (backpack, canteen, flashlight).

In addition to the searching data, the OL will need certain information critical to developing a search plan. This information must also be written on the interview form and be provided to each handler:

- Point last seen (PLS): the OL should physically inspect the PLS rather than rely on a point marked on the map (which may be incorrect) and should attempt to see things from the victim's viewpoint. If the missing person is a four-year-old child, the OL should get down to the approximate eye level of someone that small. Is there an inviting opening in the brush a taller person might not see? The OL should also determine the direction in which a person could disappear from sight most quickly ("I only turned my back for a minute and she was gone").
- Time last seen.
- Weather at time of loss (for example, did the rain that raised the creek so it could not be crossed occur before or after the person was lost).
- Subject category and/or activity when lost: child, elderly, hunter, hiker, mushroom picker, etc.
- Physical or mental condition: heart problem, diabetes, depressed.
- Terrain: barriers, escape routes, etc.

Conducting Interviews

Your unit may have one or more interviewers, depending upon its size and the capability of your personnel. While this task will often fall to the OL, other unit members should be capable of conducting interviews when more than one witness is to be questioned.

Because there can be so much information, do not reach conclusions before you have all the data. Conduct all interviews on a one-on-one basis, away from the crowd. The last thing you want is someone constantly interrupting with, "That's not the way it happened." Others will have a chance to present their version during a separate interview. Determining what is fact and what is not when faced with several versions can be a difficult task. You must sort through the data and make a judgment call.

In all your interviews, be considerate. This may be your hundredth search, but it is probably the family's first. Behave in a calm, professional manner tempered with a friendly, sympathetic attitude. Even though you may be anxious to get teams into the field, act as though you have all the time in the world. Pleasant patience can make the interview easier for both you and the person you are questioning.

Be well prepared before starting any interview. Know what information you expect to receive from each person, what information you must have to plan your search, and strive to ensure accuracy. You cannot keep repeating, "Are you *sure* she was wearing a blue blouse?"—but you would be surprised how often the person is wearing a different color blouse than described when found.

Each person to be interviewed presents special opportunities and problems.

The operational leader must plan the search based on data from interviews, victim behavior statistics and terrain analyses.
Tony Novack

A rushing stream may present an obvious barrier that would stop or "funnel" the lost person.
Bill Syrotuck

129

Family Members. These people are under a tremendous amount of stress, whether they show it or not. Some may seem very calm, while others will be very agitated. Because interviewing is an ongoing process, your interviewer should be prepared to handle a wide range of emotions during the course of a search.

Friends. If friends were the last to see the person, particularly if the disappearance occurred during a group outing, be *sure* to interview each separately. They may have worked out a story among themselves and the individual interviews may bring out inconsistencies. When conducting these interviews, do not assume that there was any wrongdoing in their activity; they may simply be frightened that they will be blamed for the incident.

Witnesses. The value of witnesses depends upon many factors. Did they know the person, or did they simply see someone matching the person's description? Be cautious of information from witnesses who claim to have seen the person after the subject was reported missing, particularly if they do not actually know the person. False leads can result in wild-goose chases to areas far from the primary search site and spread resources so thin that they lose effectiveness. While such sightings should not be immediately dismissed, neither should they be allowed to instantly alter your original search plan. Continue your coverage until you have something concrete or suggest the use of other resources to follow up on such leads.

Agency Personnel. These can include those in law enforcement (including park rangers), rescue squads, fire departments, etc.

Law enforcement officers generally have primary responsibility for the search and they are often walking encyclopedias. If they have been in their job for many years and/or were raised in the area, their knowledge will be invaluable. They will frequently know if the person has a history of mental or physical problems, if there has been trouble within the family or if the whole episode is totally out of character. They also will have access to the more unusual information you need, such as determining the weather at the time of loss by contacting the local weather bureau or the effects of a medication through contact with a hospital.

Law enforcement personnel will usually be extremely cooperative because they asked for your help and it is rare for an agency to withhold critical information from a unit whose assistance they specifically requested.

Rescue squad and fire department personnel can also be extremely helpful. If they have looked for the person before, they will be more than happy to tell you where they found him last time and where they think he might be this time. Like the law enforcement officers, they live in the community and have a very effective "grapevine." Much of the input from this group is more likely to be heard over a cup of coffee than through a formal interview and an astute base operator can gather this information during casual conversation. Always bear in mind that some of these people, who are often volunteers themselves, may feel some resentment at outsiders being brought in to do what they consider *their* job. Respect their opinions and suggestions.

The interview provides critical data, but other factors (terrain features, for instance) also have an impact. Regardless of any other planning data, however, your interviewing must be thorough. A search begins with information and proceeds on the constant input of more information. You cannot get half the answers and expect to solve the problem. A successful search begins with successful interviews.

MAPS

Having a topographical map available on every search is not always easy. Your unit should consider purchasing maps for your local search area through the U.S. Geological Survey so that you will have the original and copies available immediately upon call-out.

If you do not have unit-provided maps, you will have to rely upon the agency to obtain the necessary maps (including copies for the handlers). You should state this need during the first telephone contact prior to the unit's departure for the search. If an agency is unsure where to obtain topo maps, you might suggest the county zoning office or similar local agency that uses such maps for surveys, etc. In those cases where the agency cannot provide a topo map, you may have to rely on the less satisfactory aerial photographic or county road map. Handlers will have to utilize all their mapping skills to be effective when using these maps.

When working from an agency-provided map, check in the lower right corner for the date when it was last photo-revised, as some old maps will not show recent development or new roads. Older maps are still useful, but you must be aware of possible changes that could affect your search plan. Local people familiar with the area can usually tell you where the changes are and these should be marked on both your base map overlay and on the handlers' maps.

Before the search can begin, a search strategy must be devised.

11

Conducting the Search

ONCE ALL THE INFORMATION is collected, the operational leader will be prepared to plan the search strategy. Any such plan must be with the approval of the agency. You must never overlook the fact that they have ultimate control—and responsibility—for the search. Some agencies may relinquish control to the unit and not interfere in your decisions. Others may insist that you search certain areas, even though you feel those areas are low probability. In either case, it is the agency's decision. If you must search what you consider unlikely areas, do so without complaint. If you react to their requests with courtesy and a positive attitude, they will become far more likely to invite your suggestions as the search progresses.

PLANNING THE SEARCH

The OL should study all terrain features shown on the map that may impact on the victim's route of travel. Are there any major barriers that would either be impassable or so obvious that the person would follow them (major roads, lakes, cliffs)? What about minor barriers that could be crossed (small roads, an old fence, a small creek)? Are there any "confusion factors," such as obliterated trail markers or subtle terrain changes? Is there anything that might funnel the victim in one direction, such as a drainage or connecting clearings? Is there anything that would trap the person, such as an area with a funneling drainage with sides that become progressively steeper and end in a sheer wall?

The operational leader briefs unit members prior to teams entering the field.

Tony Campion

Dogs from a Maine search unit wait patiently while handlers study a map of the search area.

Sally Thibault

As each of these possibilities is assessed, the victim behavior statistics must be borne in mind. If there are three drainages, which would fit the median distance traveled by a person in this victim's category? If most victims in this category are found downhill (people rarely turn around to go back uphill once they have started down), which slope would lend itself best to the category statistics?

All members attend a unit briefing to discuss the proposed search. During this briefing, they will be given the information gathered to this point. All handlers should have maps of their areas or be prepared to draw them from the base camp map. The agency may be present for part of the unit briefing to provide information and input to the planning process, as well as answer any questions.

Based on all the information gathered, the OL will select prime areas to be searched and present them during the briefing. When assigning dog/handler teams, the OL must consider the strengths and weaknesses of each to ensure that the less-experienced teams are given sectors they can easily handle. If handlers express keen interest in a particular area, they should be allowed to search that area. A decision may also be made as to the type of immediate search to be conducted—hasties or sector assignments. While both may be utilized at the same time, current conditions often dictate which would be most appropriate.

BEGINNING THE SEARCH

Ideally, the unit should be ready to begin searching within one hour of arrival (although one or two handlers may be instructed to begin hasty searches much earlier). Within that time frame, all interviews, planning and unit organization should be completed.

If you arrive early in the day and handlers are well rested, you may begin with sector assignments. If, however, it is night and the unit has driven several hours, the best approach may be a hasty search of potential escape or funneling routes. Any area hasty searched at night must be included in sector search plans for daylight.

Hasty Searching

The nighttime hasty serves as an initial terrain evaluation from which can come important planning data. Each handler will be expected to give a detailed report on features found during a hasty. Perhaps an area that seemed to have high potential on the map will be placed in a lower priority because the handler reports it full of thick, impassable briers. Old trails not shown on the map may be discovered, marked on the handler's map for future reference and quickly searched. Hasties of an area's periphery can prove particularly

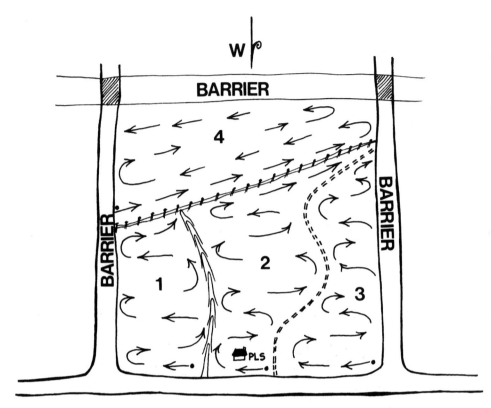

Primary search area as determined by major barriers; obvious boundaries are used to divide area into sectors.   *Linda Warshaw*

Hasty search technique, with handlers working escape or funneling routes (trail, drainage and power line).   *Linda Warshaw*

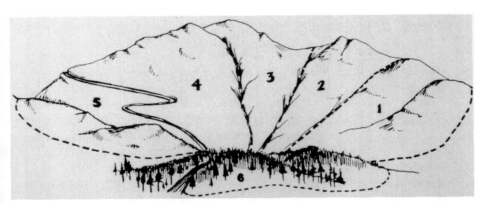

Large search area divided into sectors.

Jean Syrotuck Whittle

useful to a handler in initially surveying an area scheduled to be searched more thoroughly at daylight.

When at all possible, night searches (by hasties and/or sectors) *should* be conducted. Victims are far less likely to be moving in the dark (while they may doze, it is unlikely they will sleep; therefore, they may well respond to someone calling their name). Additionally, the cooler evening air produces better scenting conditions and, since dogs are one of the most effective tools for night searching, they should be utilized. The victim's chances of survival can decline rapidly and time is of the essence.

Care of the Returning Teams

When handlers return to base, they will be individually debriefed by the OL. Their route through their assigned area must be marked on the base map overlay and they should give their estimation of coverage. All major terrain features should be detailed, particularly if they change an area's priority. All data received from the returning handlers will be compiled and added to the overall strategy.

Base camp personnel should ensure that food and drink are available when handlers return from the field and that overnight lodging arrangements have been made. Units must be adaptable since they may be housed in anything from a nice motel to the county jail. Remote search locations rarely offer such luxury and unit members must be prepared to use their tents.

Before the unit's operation is suspended for the night, a group debriefing should be held to develop a preliminary search plan for the next day based on handler input. Base camp personnel must ensure that any additional information they may have developed is included in this debriefing. As with the earlier briefing, the agency may be present. Any information handlers have that is speculative can be aired later when only unit members are present. The agency must be advised of the overall search plan, but there will be some situations that call for discussions restricted to within the unit.

CONTINUING THE SEARCH

On each full day of searching, a unit briefing must be held prior to any team entering the field. This must provide all handlers with any new information developed and explain the overall search plan for the day. Each team must be absolutely certain of sector boundaries and supplied with a map.

During the part of the unit briefing when the agency is present, the OL may be asked to suggest nondog areas where local volunteers can be used. The agency may find itself facing 100 impatient people who want to join the search, but be reluctant to commit them for fear of interfering with the dogs. The OL must be prepared to assist in determining the best application of these resources.

Training on different vehicles pays off as dog team prepares for transport to sector on snowcat.
Jeff Doran

The search dog may find itself transported in unusual ways. This dog prefers window seat.
Penny Sullivan

Some volunteers can be utilized as stationary lookouts posted at strategic places along roads, power lines and other possible escape routes. By positioning themselves to see a fairly long distance in either direction, they will be in an ideal place to spot the victim who wanders out of the woods. Others can drive vehicles along perimeter roads, serving the same purpose on a moving basis. Both uses contain the search area so that the victim will be seen and stopped before going farther and getting into deeper trouble.

Other volunteers can be used to check possible attractions. Elderly people who have been raised in the area often, during times of confusion, talk about "going home." They are usually referring to the place where they spent their childhood. Volunteers can check those locations on a periodic basis.

Fairly open areas with good visibility can be grid searched by volunteers, while dog teams check those areas where the dog's scenting ability may be the only way to locate the victim. Four-wheel drive groups can be used to run logging roads and to transport searchers. There are numerous ways to use local volunteers without risking interference with the dogs. Both the agency and the volunteers will appreciate the "we're all in this together" attitude.

As soon as the preliminary briefing ends, handlers should enter the field. Because they will depend on their radio for hours, a radio check between each handler and base should be done before the handler leaves.

Although the handlers are capable of working by themselves, it may be advisable for someone to accompany them, particularly if a sector is extremely rugged. Unit trainees can and should be used for this purpose as the experience they gain will prove invaluable when they become operational. If family members or friends of the victim wish to go with handlers, serious consideration should be given to such requests if they are equipped and competent. It may be better to have them accompany trained searchers rather than wander around on their own.

Locals who are very familiar with the search area can be extremely helpful and should be utilized if they offer to work with a handler.

Many times a law enforcement agency will provide an officer to work with each handler. Most officers are willing to follow the handler's direction and soon adopt the team as their own, remaining with that team throughout the search.

Handlers always have the ultimate responsibility for coverage of their sectors and must ensure that those accompanying them remain close *behind* them and adhere to the handler's instructions.

A base camp operator must, of course, remain at the radio 100 percent of the time, maintaining an accurate log of each radio transmission and of each handler's progress. The BCO will frequently be visited by the agency, family members, neighbors, other searchers and the media. The media must be referred to the agency for *all* information about the search. Speculation to a reporter or unwittingly revealing information the agency wanted kept quiet would be disastrous to the unit's reputation as a professional organization. If reporters ask general questions about the unit itself, the BCO can either answer them or, if extremely busy, politely offer to arrange an interview when the OL returns from the field. Family members, too, should have limited access to radio transmissions so that any bad news can be broken to them in an appropriate manner rather than hearing it over the radio.

If the interference from onlookers is too great, the BCO may request help from the agency in securing the area. The BCO walks a delicate line between being totally cut off from everyone, thereby perhaps missing an important bit of information, and being overrun. The use of a properly instructed trainee as a base assistant will help reduce some of these problems.

CLUES

A clue can be a piece of clothing, a candy wrapper, a footprint, etc. Untrained searchers often overreact to finding a clue before its connection to the subject is proven. An anxious family may be sent on an emotional roller coaster by searchers who excitedly proclaim they have found the subject's footprint, only to later learn it did not belong to the person at all.

Any report of clues should be subdued and cautious, with the information kept between the unit and the agency until its validity can be determined. A special code should be used to radio the discovery of a potential clue in order to avoid raising false hopes among bystanders.

All clues should be flagged and left as found, unless their removal is authorized by the agency. The BCO must immediately mark the location of a clue on the base map. If it is *positively* identified as belonging to the victim, the clue and its location will become the new point last seen since it is obvious that the person has been in the area. This will in all probability have a major impact on your search plan.

THE UNIT FIND

Whether you are on your first search or your fiftieth, there is no sense of accomplishment quite like a unit find. When the dog performs exactly as in training, with a strong alert, close-in, recall/refind, the handler will understand why all the hours of work were so necessary. Regardless of which dog makes the find, the entire unit will share the handler's feeling of pride.

Handlers must be prepared to cope with any situation involving the victim. If the person is alive and well, evacuation may be nothing more than leading the individual back to base. If the person is ill or injured, the handler's first-aid and evacuation skills will be called upon. In either case, assistance may be required from base camp. A person who is physically well may manifest emotional problems, either from the trauma of being lost or from problems that may have led him to become "lost" in the first place (such as

Handlers should assume evidence may be in area around a "find" and avoid disturbing the immediate vicinity. *Penny Sullivan*

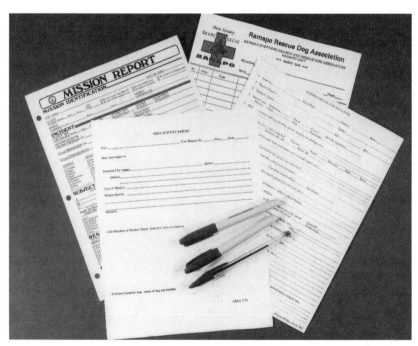

All searches should be recorded on documents, including interview forms, mission reports and radio logs. *Peggy Williams*

depression, possibly to the extent of being suicidal). In those cases, the handler may have to literally coax the person into returning home or request that the base send a family member, agency representative or someone else the person trusts.

If the victim is deceased, the handler should proceed on the assumption that there is evidence in the area that the agency will need to determine the cause of death. In an obvious case of violent death, preservation of the scene is critical as foul play may be involved. When rewarding the dog after finding a deceased victim, the handler should take it far enough away to avoid disturbing the area and any evidence it may contain.

All handlers must be mentally prepared to deal with the sight of a deceased subject. The actions of the dog will give advance notice that someone is in the vicinity and the handler should begin to emotionally prepare for the possibility of finding a body.

When making a find, the handler must radio the grid coordinates and subject's condition to the base, along with any request for assistance. Base must record the coordinates on the map and the *exact* time on the radio log. If there is foul play involved, all this information may be required by the agency in the event of a criminal trial. The handler must also note everything possible about the scene and be prepared to describe the dog's performance, as handlers are sometimes required to testify as witnesses during a trial.

The ARDA has a general policy of not revealing the names of the dog and handler making the find to the news media. This policy is based on the knowledge that any operational team is capable of making the find and it is a matter of chance which handler was assigned to the correct area. All finds are considered a successful unit effort, not the sole accomplishment of one dog or handler.

SUSPENDING THE MISSION

Obviously, the successful mission ends when the missing person is found. On many occasions, however, your unit will face the decision to suspend without finding the subject. It is never easy, but circumstances often dictate when you will have to head home.

1. All logical areas have been searched. If you have spent three days on the scene and thoroughly searched several square miles, there may simply be no logical place left to cover. This should be a joint decision with the agency, or the agency may independently decide to end the effort.

2. New information is received indicating the subject has left the area. As with a clue, suspending the search must be based on fact rather than rumor. Again, the agency will make the final decision, depending upon their assessment of the information's reliability.

3. Unit members must return home or to work. The commitment time should have been explained to the agency when the unit was first contacted and most agencies understand that members have other responsibilities. If some members can stay for an extra day or two, the agency may welcome their presence; if the OL must leave, suggestions for new search areas should be left with the agency and the handlers.

If you must suspend your efforts even though the subject has not been found, it is a relatively frequent practice for units to offer to train in the area on weekends if the search site is not too far from home. Such training must be conducted with the agency's permission for reasons both of professional courtesy and legalities (to avoid problems with trespassing, for instance).

DOCUMENTATION

You will need to document all aspects of each mission. Such documents provide written records in case a legal question is raised as to the conduct of the search and enable you to accurately critique the mission. Documentation should include:

1. Radio logs showing the nature of each transmission with the handler's unit number, the time and grid coordinates.
2. Interview sheets.
3. Maps showing the handlers' routes through their sectors, the boundaries of each sector, probabilities of detection, where there were alerts, and where clues and/or the subject was found.
4. A mission report form that includes weather (temperature and conditions, such as rain or snow), wind direction and velocity, type(s) of terrain, the name of the requesting agency with a contact number and individual, subject category and how the mission was concluded (if the subject was found, by whom and how far from the PLS). You may want to include a list of other resources used by the agency, such as mounted searchers, helicopters, grid searchers, etc. The report should also show the names of unit members who responded and how many days they were on the search.

A separate folder should be maintained on each mission for ready reference. Such complete documentation will aid your study of victim behavior and the effects of weather, wind and terrain on the dog's scenting ability.

12

Special Applications

$\mathbf{O}$NCE YOU HAVE trained your dog for air scenting, it can be used on a wide variety of difficult searches. This chapter includes training techniques for some of the more unusual missions where your assistance may be requested.

WATER SEARCH TRAINING

Before starting this training, the handler should understand water currents, tides, deposition zones, thermoclines, underwater contours and depths and their resulting effect on scent.

The best area to begin water training is a privately owned pond or a private part of a lake with no bystanders or nearby neighbors to cause conflicting scent. If there are people in the area, be sure that they remain downwind of the working area (this also applies on actual searches).

Although some work will be done in shallow water near the shore, the ideal water depth is generally ten to twelve feet. This will minimize surface disturbance and maximize good scent flow. All training should be done with divers to ensure a reliable source of human scent.

You will need a diver who is thoroughly briefed on how the dogs work, both from a boat and from shore. The diver will advise you of the best way to give a "surface" signal, as you want to surface the diver quickly to reinforce the dog as soon after the alert as possible. Divers may or may not wear wetsuits, as the dogs will be able to detect them either way.

Perhaps of most concern to handlers is the diver's air tank, which periodically emits bubbles to the surface and may give away the diver's location. Because there is often no choice but to use these tanks, handlers must avoid inadvertently training the dog to respond to this visual clue and must instead encourage it to react to the airborne scent only.

Divers who are relatively close to the surface will emit large, intermittent bubbles in concert with their breathing, thereby increasing the possibility of inadvertently cueing the dog. However, the pressure in deeper water affects the diver's exhaled air by causing the rising bubbles to expand until they break into smaller bubbles that create far less surface disturbance. Obviously, the deeper the diver, the less distracting the bubbles. If the diver is in very shallow water, a snorkel may be a solution to this problem.

For the initial introduction to water detection, it is advisable to start each dog with the runaway game, where the dog is allowed to watch the diver enter the water. (Very young dogs can be worked by their owners, who can wade into the water and hide behind reeds, a bush or lie in the water if it is warm enough.)

For this training, a gradual offshore slope is ideal so that the dog does not have to swim to reach the diver. While all search dogs must know how to swim, the purpose of this session is a quick, easy find. The diver should carry the ball or stick, showing it to the dog as an enticement just before wading into the water. The dog can then be released on the "find" command and allowed to race out to the diver. The ensuing play session can be carried out onshore to ensure that the dog receives a strong, prolonged reward.

Advanced dogs with actual search experience often do not need this introduction, as they will react to human scent regardless of its source. For intermediate dogs who are given runaway problems, once or twice should be enough. These dogs should be nearly mission-ready and should quickly understand what is expected of them. If a dog does not respond eagerly, advanced work should not be attempted until it is successfully completing these problems.

The next step is a shoreline search without the dog watching the diver leave. The diver should be totally submerged just offshore. Again, such a shore problem enables the handler to give the dog an immediate, enthusiastic play session, which will not be possible during later advanced work in the confines of a boat. These reward sessions will be critical in maintaining the dog's interest, and full advantage should be taken of the reward opportunities presented by shore problems.

Once the dog is eagerly indicating the diver's location from shore, it can progress to work in the boat. Selection of the boat for this training session should consider safety factors, as well as the dog's comfort so it can concentrate on the search problem. The boat should be low, close to the water, stable and maneuverable.

It is acceptable for the handler to allow the dog to watch as the diver either swims or is taken by boat to deeper water. The diver may call to the dog

Dogs should be introduced to divers prior to training so their "unusual appearance" will not startle
the animal.   *Bob Snyder*

Dog alerts toward diver during a shore problem.   *Bob Snyder*

During more advanced training, dogs are allowed to watch divers leave for deeper water.
Penny Sullivan

When working from a boat, the dog should stand or sit upright with an alert, working attitude.
Penny Sullivan

Dog alerts on diver by dipping its nose to the water.

Peter Bremy

Diver rewards dog with stick.

Peter Bremy

or make a motion to attract its attention before disappearing under the water. The handler should verbally increase the dog's interest in what the diver is doing: "Where's he going? Look at that!" If one boat is used to transport the diver and carry the dog, it should return to shore quickly to pick up the dog whose interest will be at its peak. A dog that squeaks and whines to go after the diver is exhibiting maximum motivation and must be allowed to work while its eagerness is high.

At this point, the boat operator becomes a critical player who must understand how wind and water currents affect the dog's ability to pick up scent and be able to maneuver the boat accordingly. The handler must know the diver's location at this stage and should concentrate only on the dog to observe its individual alert.

On the first problem, the operator should put the boat directly downwind of the diver so the still enthusiastic dog can hit the scent quickly. The dog should be sitting or standing upright in the front of the boat where it can pick up all the air currents washing over the bow. A dog that rides with its head hanging over one side may miss the scent coming from the front or other side. Such a close scan is unnecessary and, by limiting the scenting scope of the dog, may even prolong the search. The handler should be sitting behind the dog, relaxed yet encouraging. A leash may or may not be used, depending upon the conditions.

It is here that the handler will learn to read the dog and must pay close attention. Some dogs bark and try to jump out of the boat; some lean over the side of the boat, often biting at the water; some simply lift their noses and keep them in that position until they have lost the scent.

Once the dog alerts, the diver should be surfaced by the prearranged signal. The diver can either have the dog's ball or stick or can take it from the handler upon surfacing and then give it to the dog. As with the runaway game, this problem with the visual cue of watching the diver leave only needs to be practiced once or twice with the intermediate or advanced dog.

The next step is the final preparation for an actual mission. The dog will not be allowed to see the diver disappear and the handler will not know the diver's location. The boat operator, who *must* know the diver's location, will be requested to work on a grid pattern back and forth, downwind of the search area, with the handler gauging the width of sweeps based on the wind velocity and estimated detection distance. The boat operator must be in a position to advise of any subtle alerts the handler might miss.

This is a learning experience for both the dog and handler, and the boat operator will again be a critical link in making sure the dog succeeds. The entire exercise can be ruined by an operator who remains silent and continues a search pattern long after they have passed the diver. If a dog is taken through an area, alerts repeatedly and gets no reward because the handler fails to read it properly, it will soon either lose interest or decide it is the wrong scent. This same problem of lost interest will occur on real missions. The best solution is to mark the alert area after one or two sweeps and then have at least one other dog taken through the area to see if it, too, indicates scent.

On a training problem, however, the purpose is to reinforce and reward the dog, not see how long it stays interested in the scent. If the operator notes an alert based on prior knowledge of the diver's location but the handler misses or misreads it, the operator should advise the handler. After a few such problems, the handler should become very adept at reading the dog. That skill is the essence of success on search missions and must be developed by practice.

It is an inescapable fact that much of the polishing can only be done on real missions. Many drownings occur where underwater debris and/or currents make a training simulation impossible. Once the dog has successfully worked training problems, however, it will generally indicate human scent regardless of the circumstances. Practice should also continue with the dog working from shore since water conditions on searches may preclude the use of a boat.

Handlers should practice problems where the dog is worked on divers from directions other than downwind. Bringing the dogs in from all four directions has frequently proven highly effective in pinpointing more accurately the victim's location. Attention must also be paid to the difference between an alert on scent residue, which is often encountered in deposition zones (areas along river shorelines downstream of the subject's location), and alerts on the subject. The residue alerts are usually much less pronounced than those on the subject.

The difficulties of drowning missions lie in two areas: (1) pinpointing the source of the scent because of water or current drift, and (2) adequately rewarding the dog. To be successful in pinpointing scent, the handler must be educated to the nuances of wind, water currents and thermoclines, as well as the effect of debris and deposition zones.

Care must be exercised in rewarding for indications that often cannot be proven due to the difficulty of body recovery. Highly motivated dogs can survive the lack of a reward on a water search if there is any doubt, just as they do on land searches where they do not make the find. Their enthusiasm can be maintained by periodic training problems culminating in strong reward sessions.

THE "SEEK" OR "LOOK" COMMAND

When training for avalanche, disaster and article search, the "seek," "look" or "search" command should be used. Choose a word that feels comfortable to you and that does not sound like another basic command. You may decide to use a phrase rather than a single word, such as "look for it." The intent is to indicate to the dog that you wish it to use a modified form of searching.

Dog performing close, nose-to-the-ground search on "seek" or "look" command.   *Doug Stanley*

In wilderness searches, the dog has learned to search in response to the "find" command, using a wide, ranging pattern with head held high checking the wind. The scent is detectable from quite a distance and is obviously a person once the dog closes in.

In the close work often encountered where subjects may be buried or a small article is to be located, the dog must learn that it is looking for a puddle of scent on the surface that may be detectable for only very short distances downwind. When the dog closes in on a buried or concealed person, the apparent source will *not* be obvious and the dog must learn to dig down to the true source. Once it understands that the person is *below* the surface, it will quickly learn to get its nose closer to the ground and carefully scan the surface while keeping the ranging pattern closer, slower and more thorough.

When training this command for avalanche work, it is important that handlers do not condition the dog to think that all snow work is avalanche work. Looking for a missing hunter in late fall is one example. The environment is snow, but you could be looking for someone who has perched on a stump, collapsed in the shelter of some trees or perhaps fallen in the open and is now covered by a foot of new snow. This victim is certainly not buried in the debris of boulders and blocks of snow as an avalanche victim would be. Consequently, while this is definitely a snow environment, the "find" command would be much more efficient since this type of victim will emanate a large amount of scent even through snow cover. Both wilderness and avalanche searches need to be practiced in the snow, each utilizing their different techniques.

When the dog learns to respond to the command and not to the environment alone, you will find that the chosen command is useful for many applications. Consider, for example, the consequence of a bomb explosion, where a person was blown into small pieces. It was necessary for SARDA teams to retrieve as many of these pieces as possible for analytic examination to determine the cause of the explosion. The pieces were driven into the ground, plastered against the trees and, in many instances, were smaller than one-quarter square inch. The sixty pounds recovered required a thorough, nose-close-to-the-ground scanning technique and the "seek" command was used, which implied to the dog that "I want you to thoroughly scan the surface for an extremely small intensity of scent and show me its source."

If, on a wilderness search in the middle of summer, there is a suspicion that a "lost" child was murdered and buried in a shallow grave, the "seek" command could be used for scanning specific areas. The "find" command would still be used for general searching (perhaps the child really was just lost).

Article searching can be done with the same command, but you need not train for this excessively. A brief article search once a month or so will maintain the dog for use on evidence searches. Although you want a dog that will indicate articles on a wilderness search, precious time can be lost on avalanche or disaster missions if a dog indicates and digs for every article of

It is important the dog not be conditioned to think all snow work is avalanche work.

Bill Syrotuck

clothing while a victim lies nearby. A skilled handler should note and quickly check each indication by the dog, whether subtle or intense. If there is doubt, the handler can mark the site for digging parties to investigate further while the dog continues searching. Except in specifically designated evidence searches, your primary purpose is to find people.

EVIDENCE SEARCHES

An evidence search must be slow and meticulous, inspecting every inch of surface since the object sought is often very small or hidden. The dog may be searching for body fluids in the soil, small pieces of human tissue, articles that may retain scent residue (gloves, shotgun shells, wallets, etc.) or the buried body of a homicide subject.

While the dog has already been trained to indicate articles when searching for a person on the "find" command, evidence search requires the slow, nose-to-the-ground work previously described in this chapter in the "seek" command section. In addition, the hand signals for a directed wilderness search may be used to produce a quartering evidence search pattern with the dog working to either side of the handler.

Early training may be conducted by hiding the dog's favorite toy or stick (thoroughly handled to ensure strong human scent) in an obvious location. When the dog finds the object, it should be rewarded with an enthusiastic play session. Most dogs quickly understand this new game and you can progress to hiding different, well-scented articles (leather wallets or other items that hold scent, keys, etc.). The dog should be encouraged to pick the item up since the alert on a real mission may be so subtle that the handler might miss seeing the object. Eventually you should be able to hide items under leaves, in a brush pile and similar places. It is recommended that you occasionally throw the object rather than place it so that there is no track for the dog to follow. If available, human tissue can be used for training to prepare the dog for those instances when it must search for scattered remains of victims from explosions, aircraft accidents, etc. Just as with multiple-victim finds in wilderness searching, dogs should learn to search for several objects.

CRIME SCENE SEARCHES

Any search may become a criminal case. For example, at the initial briefing it is known only that a person is missing, not if a crime has been committed. A dog team then finds the missing subject, who is deceased. Unless proven otherwise, the area is to be treated as a crime scene. If the handler observes that the person appeared to die an unnatural death, look for anything suspicious about the position of the body, a weapon near the body or any details concerning the location of the body (lying on the surface of the ground, in water or covered by rocks or branches).

As the first person on the scene, the handler is responsible for protecting the area. While waiting for the authorities to arrive, do not walk unnecessarily in the immediate vicinity of the body. The general rule is: "One way in, same way out." Reward and leave the dog some distance from the scene. To avoid destroying evidence, do not pick up or touch anything! Carefully observe the area, making notes of what you see or may have seen during the search, including the times they occurred. You may later be required to testify at an inquest or before a grand jury, which will not be a time to rely upon memory. (Records maintained by base camp personnel may also be requested by the prosecutor and/or defense attorney, making accurate radio logs and map notations imperative.)

Whether the subject is alive or deceased, always remember to disturb the area as little as possible when determining the subject's condition and treating any injuries. Recovery of evidence is just as critical in the case of a living rape victim as it is with a homicide victim.

Above all, do not discuss the case with anyone other than law enforcement officers. The most innocent-looking individual may be responsible for the missing person's situation, and what seems an idle comment may provide the suspect time to remove valuable evidence. All questions pertaining to the missing subject or the search strategy must be referred to the responsible agency.

In the event a confession by a person being tried for a homicide is inadmissible, dog handlers who participated in the search may be required to testify as expert witnesses in relation to both training and search experience (written training logs should be maintained for this purpose). ARDA handlers have testified as expert witnesses to the "inevitable discovery" of a double homicide when the confession was inadmissible. In that case, dog teams were working in the direction of the bodies, which were discovered by other means. The prosecutor used the "inevitable discovery" approach to require the handlers to testify that, had they continued, the dogs would have inevitably discovered the bodies.

All crime scene searches are not necessarily for a body, but may involve only portions of human remains. In some instances, dogs can help authorities determine that a crime has *not* occurred, such as in the following case. In the course of leveling the backyard of a new home being built over the site of a burned-out hotel, a human skull was found that still had hair attached. Because this indicated a possible crime, ARDA dogs were used to search dirt piles that had already been removed and deposited in another part of the village. The dogs found the frontal portions of two different human skulls and, when searching the backyard later, alerted in a number of places. Anthropologists systematically searched the alert areas and found a complete cemetery in which bones were estimated to be 80 to 100 years old.

In another instance, dog teams were requested to search an area where a human skull had been found the day before, again indicating a possible crime scene. The medical examiner stated that a better identification could be made if the three missing front teeth could be found. The leaf-covered surface had been disturbed in looking for the skeleton. Two dogs searching the area alerted to a small pile of leaves, where the three teeth were found. The time of death was estimated to be three years prior to the body's discovery.

In both the above instances, the "seek" command was used.

When working known or possible criminal cases, the handler must be extremely professional in what is done and said. To be thorough, handlers must practice clue awareness and man-tracking skills (noting bits of paper, disturbed rocks, broken branches, etc.). The hopes of many people rest upon the teamwork of the dog and handler trained to provide answers to an already difficult case.

BODY SEARCHING

Well-trained air-scenting dogs have proven highly effective in locating human remains weeks or even months after the subject's death. While your hope is to save lives, locating a deceased subject eases the family's uncertainty and resolves the situation for the agency in charge.

Training Aids

The ARDA has found one proven method for training dogs to find bodies: train them well to find people. Although most handlers only have the opportunity to train on live subjects, their dogs respond eagerly and confidently to human scent even when the person is deceased. Occasionally, with an agency's permission, you may be allowed to bring nearby dogs in to acquaint them with a deceased subject. You may also be able to work sites from which a body has been removed or use soil (which retains scent) from that site. Human tissue and bones have also been used as training aids.

Our knowledge of the true components of human scent is so limited that the use of simulated or synthetic "dead" scent material is questionable. In using such substances, we may risk inadvertently training the dog to search for nonhuman chemical odors.

ARDA units never substitute dead animal parts for human scent under any circumstances, as we cannot flatly state when, or even if, a body loses its human scent. To use animal meat without real knowledge of its similarity to the scent of a human is to invite serious problems on a search. This is particularly true in disaster and drowning searches, where valuable time can be lost or divers jeopardized in attempts to recover dead dogs, deer, etc.

The Dog's Reaction to a Body

Although the dog's alert, initial close-in and recall/refind should be the same as on a live subject, inexperienced dogs will sometimes exhibit caution

Well-trained dogs have proven effective at finding human bones, including these of subject deceased several years.
Penny Sullivan

or hesitation when they are *very close* to a decomposed body. The alert distance will be the same for live or dead finds and the dog will show its normal excitement on the refind. When the inexperienced dog gets to within a foot or two of the body, however, it may stop and cautiously stretch its neck to sniff the body. Clearly, the dog senses there is something different about this person. However, *if* the dog receives its usual enthusiastic play session, it will become very reliable on both live and dead finds. Experienced dogs will complete the refind and immediately look to their handler for reward, virtually ignoring the body.

The future success of the dog relies upon positive reinforcement by the handler. An example of the damage that can be done occurred when a dog found a body and was immediately kenneled without reward due to overreaction on the part of the searchers. The dog's training was set back months and it took a great deal of effort to overcome its loss of confidence and enthusiasm. If the handler reflects negative emotions, the dog will think it has done something wrong. If, on the other hand, the dog gets an immediate reward, it will develop what Jeff Doran of SARDA described as a "feel-right attitude." The dog will know it has done something special.

Buried Subjects

Many searches are for homicide victims who are frequently in shallow graves of only a few feet. These have not necessarily presented a problem for the dog.

ARDA experiments have shown that soil retains the scent of body fluids for an extended period of time. Dogs have alerted on such sites months after the body was removed. They have also proven very effective at finding human bones.

Handlers should spend some time researching the disturbed earth that is typical of a burial site. The ground over a deep grave will frequently show a depression as a result of the ground settling as the body decomposes. Turning the soil and uprooting the original vegetation will also often create a visible difference between the grave and the immediate vicinity.

Commands

When searching for a buried body, the "seek" or "look" command should be used if you are doing a close search of a small area. In other cases, the "find" command should be given.

In 1969 Jean Syrotuck's dog made the first avalanche find by an American-trained dog.
Courtesy National Park Service

13

Avalanche Training

$\mathbf{W}$HEN PREPARING DOGS for avalanche work, training aids must be carefully selected. Unless there is no alternative, all training should be done with live "victims." The use of clothing articles is debatable. While these are certainly easier and quicker to use in training, finding the victim is of prime importance and *all* training should be oriented in that direction. When clothing is used, the dog learns to view such articles as being of equal importance as the victim if it is praised equally. On a real mission where minutes count, a dog trained in this manner may spend considerable time trying to dig up a glove near the surface, only to have the victim die fifty feet away. It is no achievement to have found fifteen articles of clothing and then find the victim too late.

Victim-oriented dogs will still indicate clothing on real missions; however, the indication from the dog will be vague. A good handler will recognize that there is probably something under the surface, but realize that it is of less importance than the victim. Regardless of the dog's reaction, however, the site should be flagged and a digging party called before the handler moves on.

Orienting the dogs to sound is of some value. The acoustics of snow are such that a victim can hear diggers or probers far easier than the probers can hear the victim. There have been instances where victims were shouting but not heard by searchers; however, a dog can quite easily hear them. Dogs can also hear the sound emitted by a SKADI (a personal locator transmitter) and can home in faster than a person trying to triangulate with a second SKADI.

PRACTICE VICTIMS AND HOLES

Being buried under several feet of snow can be unnerving to the uninitiated. Without some precautions and instruction (such as using graduated burial depths and times), practice victims may be recovered in a complete state of shock.

In the early stages of the dog's training, the practice victims are buried in shallow holes and are able to free themselves easily and quickly. As the training progresses, the victims will be buried deeper and deeper. When it is anticipated that the victims will be unable to free themselves without assistance, the following recommendations are made:

1. Holes should be dug with a pocket at each end to allow the victims to wiggle their feet and have freedom of movement in the head and shoulders. The hole should be wide enough for the victims to lie with elbows outstretched and have several inches to spare. The victims should be consulted to ensure that they do not feel the hole is too short or too narrow. The victims should *never* be allowed to enter the hole while short of breath.

2. On entry, the victims should lie on their stomachs and get into a comfortable position, then rest on their elbows and arch their backs. Blankets should be placed over them for the dog to tug.

3. The victims' feet and legs should be covered first, followed by covering along the back. After about one foot of snow has been shoveled into the hole, the victims should relax their positions to see if the snow will stay packed. Shovelers must stop while this is being done. Once it is clear that the snow will stay firm, the victims should once again arch their backs and press against the snow until the hole is completely filled in from above. This procedure should leave several inches of space between the victims' bodies and the snow when they relax. During this entire process, the shovelers should occasionally stop and ask the victims if everything is all right. The victims must remember that sound carries down through snow better than up and must yell in order to be heard.

4. Snow is added to the hole until it blends into the surrounding texture and snow level.

5. The general area should be thoroughly crisscrossed by snowshoe tracks so there is no single path leading right to the hole's location. An area twenty feet around the hole should be thoroughly turned over by shovel to ensure that the dog is not cueing on the change of snow texture.

6. Radio contact with the victims is a necessity and frequent checks should be made.

While getting comfortable in the hole, victims must make sure that there are no lumps, bumps or rocks under them. These become very irritating in

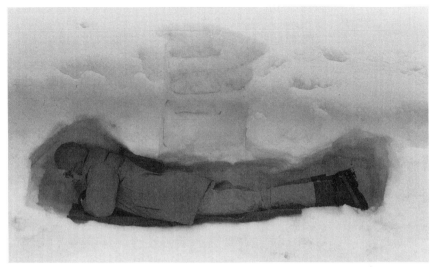

Side view of snow cave, showing size of hole and victim placement.   *Bill Syrotuck*

The dog should be encouraged to dig eagerly when it locates the victim.   *Bill Syrotuck*

short order. Being unable to do anything about them further adds to the feeling of being encased in cement. Victims should also be well insulated against the cold because they are immobile. Taking a book and light will help the time pass quickly. People who have not played victim before will be surprised how light it is inside the hole and handlers should reassure them that they are not going into a deep, dark dungeon.

The use of screens, boards, ski poles, etc., as a roof for the hole is discouraged. Dogs, in the process of digging, may pierce their pads on sharp points or get their paws caught in screen mesh. Such an experience will make them very reluctant to dig in the future. Caution must also be exercised when working a very loosely packed hole, as a dog that falls into one that is four or five feet deep may become very leery of holes.

While it may seem that the deeper the practice victims, the more difficult the problem is for the dog, time lapse may be as important as depth. A person buried in a shallow hole for ten minutes may emit the same amount of scent as a person buried ten feet would emit after thirty minutes. Consequently, it is not always necessary to use deep holes to create a good training problem for the dog. Shallow holes of two to three feet should not always be used, either, as the dog can frequently tell when it has stepped on the victim and be cued by feel rather than scent. SARDA found that five feet of snow above the victim is sufficient for advanced dogs *providing* the time from burial to release of the dog is short. Under these conditions, the dog's task is to differentiate between the scent intensities of those who buried the person and of the victim. Since the time lapse is short, the intensity of scent at the surface will be very small.

Having the scents of others in the area cannot be avoided. Since this exists in every practice session, it becomes a challenge for the dog to detect the very low intensity of the victim's scent coming up through the snow and discriminate that scent from those around it.

Holes should only be used once as the disturbed snow and surrounding scents would serve as an obvious cue for a second dog.

GROUP PRACTICE SESSIONS

It is recommended that multiple holes be dug (about three per dog) in advance. A series of short, repeated successful performances is more beneficial than a single difficult one and, therefore, all holes must be dug in one session. The holes should cover a wide area so that one set can be used by one dog without interfering with the performance of another. After all the holes have been dug, the victims should wait an hour or so before being placed to allow dispersion of the diggers' scents. The amount of time it takes to prepare these holes will depend upon the number of people available to help, but enough time should be allotted in the day's schedule for this to be accomplished.

A Georgia search dog digging for victim in soft dirt, which is ideal for training this response for both avalanche and disaster work. *Sandy Crain*

Handlers should help the dog dig as the victim may be only a foot below the surface. *Bill Syrotuck*

165

The session should begin with the burial of victims in several adjacent holes (three is ideal). The number of diggers should be a minimum of two. After the victims are buried and the appropriate time has passed, the dog is released and its training commences. After the dog successfully finds the first victim, the exercise is immediately repeated on the second and third victims. If the area is large enough, a second set of victims can be buried downwind while the first dog is working. The principle to be kept in mind is that the tempo of training should be quick with successful and rapid performances that are immediately rewarded.

ALERTING AND DISPATCHING

Having fully tested and trained avalanche dogs stationed at a ski area is ideal. Practically speaking, however, the odds of an avalanche at any given American ski area are so low and the occurrences so sporadic that it is often more appropriate to utilize a dog unit with all-around capabilities. Your unit may have to service five or six ski areas from one central location, which means handlers must be rapidly contacted and dispatched.

There will always be some time lag. If the ski area is forty miles away, it may be one hour from the time of call-out until the dog arrives on scene. Since victim survival times are so short, other rescue attempts (such as probe lines) will be initiated before your arrival. If the person has not been found by these means, the dog will be the best asset, even though you have to wait up to ten minutes to allow dispersal of scent from previous searches. There is always a chance that the victim is still alive and you must perform accordingly.

A general alerting system for the unit has already been described in Chapter 8. Avalanche work requires an even faster response. Teams should be in a constant state of readiness during high avalanche hazard conditions. Liaison should be established with local military or private helicopter facilities, with handlers aware of potential landing sites near their homes (such as a schoolyard or parking lot free of power lines and other hazards).

A "state of readiness" means the following:

1. Handlers have immediate access to the telephone; their gear is packed and ready to go.
2. During working hours, handlers will take their dogs and equipment to work with them. If necessary, dogs can be left in the car, but obviously they should be checked occasionally.
3. During nonworking hours, the handlers should inform the coordinator of their whereabouts and contact number if they must leave home for any reason. If no telephone number can be provided, the handler must check in every hour or so. Beepers or pagers should be considered as handlers would then be freed from the telephone and still remain in contact.

When an avalanche call is received, many tend to think in terms of responding by helicopter. However, only part of the unit should be transported by this means, with the remainder responding by vehicle. Prime avalanche weather is often adverse for flying and a helicopter may be grounded, then turned back or unable to land due to inclement weather. Teams traveling by car may require a police escort as heavy traffic may delay the teams so much that valuable time is lost.

WORKING AN AVALANCHE MISSION

There is a common misconception that the area should be sterile before avalanche dogs can be used. Actually, the dogs can be used even after a probe team has gone through the area provided at least ten minutes are allowed for the scent to disperse. All probe teams and other assistance must be positioned downwind from the area as the dogs work to preclude scent interference.

Digging parties of at least three per party should be formed and equipped with probes and shovels. They should be stationed downwind from the dogs, ready to rush to a point indicated by the dog and start digging once the handler has marked it. Handlers should carry a number of wands or similar marking devices.

Each dog develops a distinctive alerting and digging response. The handler will normally see a nose alert, followed by checking for a precise place to begin digging. The dog will then stop and poke its nose into the snow, checking for the best direction, and then begin digging with great enthusiasm and perseverance, possibly whining at the same time.

There are times when the dog will not indicate in its usual keen manner. Its reactions may be somewhat vague and indefinite; it appears to hunt around more and its digging may be tentative or nonexistent. You may realize that the dog has made an indication but be unable to tell if it is the very faint scent of a victim or the strong scent of a mitt (which the dog may ignore after some investigation). Since you cannot take the chance of making an error, you should mark the spot and proceed on your search pattern, leaving the questionable area to be searched by the digging party.

The handler should not be surprised if the dog indicates four or five different places in an avalanche area. This is especially true with slab avalanches where the scent may move horizontally or at angles and then leak out to the surface in several different places. The dog may give several medium to strong alerts, appearing very interested and persistent but having trouble following through with intensive digging. At this point, the handler should evaluate the geography of the snow and cracks. The most efficient approach is to move off, have the area dug through, and then bring the dog back a short time later in an attempt to determine a direction.

All handlers should have radios. When working an avalanche, the handler should occasionally report on the dog's progress. If a dog becomes

Dogs expected to work avalanche missions must learn to accept transport on ski lifts.
Bill Syrotuck

168

fatigued or is not working well, a replacement team can be summoned with a minimum of delay.

The tempo of the entire mission should be rapid: work quickly and thoroughly, mark an indication, call for a digging party, move on, mark, call the digging party, move—every second counts. If the dog starts digging in earnest, get on your hands and knees and start digging, too. The victim may be a foot below the surface.

Handlers must always be aware of the potential for more avalanches. They should preplan escape paths and be prepared to respond quickly upon receiving an avalanche warning.

Night avalanche work creates its own hazards. Close contact with each handler must be maintained as impending avalanches can only be heard, not seen, and by the time the noise reaches the handler it may be too late.

Night searching should be done with headlamps, which will leave both hands free. Marking can be done with wands that have reflective tape wound around them so that they can be easily spotted by the digging party (although even a flashlight stuck in the snow will serve the purpose).

Your attitude will reflect in the performance of the dog. If you lack confidence, the dog will know and feel it. If you are unsteady or unnerved, the dog will be too. Your lack of confidence in yourself, your dog or the situation will result in a poor performance by both of you. Go into such a mission well trained and with a strong positive attitude of "I'll find the person if humanly possible," and you will. Your own attitude may save a life.

A European rescue dog has the "bringsel stick" attached to its collar, which it takes in its mouth when it finds the victim. This is a signal to the handler that the dog is on alert.

Bill Syrotuck

14

Disaster Training

$\mathbf{T}$HE TERM *disaster* can bring to mind a multitude of images. It may apply to numerous situations, either natural or man-made: devastating earthquakes that topple entire cities; raging flood waters that break levees and swamp whole towns; a gas leak that destroys a single-family dwelling; a major train derailment; the total havoc wreaked by tornadoes; the tragic scattered ruins of a broken jumbo jet.

THE MISSION

Whatever the event, it is usually sudden, calamitous and very often involves a number of human victims. Dog teams may be requested to search for possible survivors buried beneath tons of debris or to help with body recovery efforts over a large expanse of ground. Missing subjects may be alive and trapped, possibly badly injured, or the subjects may be deceased and widely scattered. In addition to the myriad scents and contamination present in most disaster areas, the sought-after human remains may be charred or decomposing.

Hazards abound for both dog and handler: hanging debris above and shifting rubble below; gas leaks, toxic smoke and spills; open electrical circuits; hidden fires; razor-sharp edges; suffocating dust; deep, miring mud. Improvisation and common sense will be the rule. Obviously, every site must be approached with caution. Disaster search must be slow and deliberate, with safety uppermost in every searcher's thoughts.

Disaster search can never be a one-man show. Many resources are involved. When dealing with collapsed structures, search dog teams must work closely with heavy-rescue specialists experienced in trench and confined space rescue, structural experts and medical trauma teams. For the sake of everyone, victims and search personnel alike, it is crucial that each member of the team realize their limitations as well as abilities and recognize the interdependence of all. It is probably nowhere better illustrated than in disasters that the dog is truly just one resource, highly efficient and often invaluable, but only one part of the total effort.

Safety for the rescuers must always be paramount. Handlers should be familiar with the possible dangers through field and classroom training in such topics as hazardous material and basic rescue procedures, and through joint training sessions with other disaster resources. Most such courses are for familiarization only. In the field, the handler must continually rely upon the knowledge of others, especially for building assessment, proper shoring techniques and other safety procedures. If the structural safety specialists say ''Stay out,'' they mean it! Do not endanger yourself, your dog or possibly others by engaging in unnecessary risk taking. Your job is to work as an integral team, to save and *protect* lives.

The dog and handler will work in strike teams, usually consisting of four dog/handler teams and a leader. Within the strike-team configuration, the dog/handler teams may be further split into groups of two in order to facilitate the buddy safety system. As one team works, the second handler keeps watch, not only to catch a fleeting alert the working dog's handler may miss, but also to spot possible dangers and provide assistance or call for help if needed. Each handler should have a radio for communication to the surface and the strike-team leader, especially once the team begins working beneath the rubble.

Handlers generally wear highly visible jumpsuits that are nonrestrictive, protective and have little opportunity to become snagged (they should be equipped with zippered pockets). Hardhats (with chin straps and very little brim), heavy work gloves and good boots are also required. Unlike wilderness search, very little is carried on site as every bulge can prove a danger. Small radios, in slings or special pockets, and flashlights or headlamps are essential. Small canteens of water for your dog and protective dust masks for you should also be carried.

DISASTER WORK METHODS

Generally speaking, the dog will work off lead, without collar, harness or other encumbrances. It is essential that the animal be accustomed to ''scruff holds'' and being pushed and pulled from place to place. There are times when a sling and safety line may be required for the dog's own safety. There may also be situations where the team will need to be raised or lowered into

The destruction left by a major earthquake is obvious in this picture from Soviet Armenia.
Penny Sullivan

ARDA team searches for victims of 1985 Puerto Rican mudslides.   *Bob Langendoen*

position with available rope systems. All of this must, of course, be practiced in advance as part of the team's training.

Disaster work will be an extension of the dog's basic wilderness search training. As in water or avalanche search, though the environment may be different, the principles remain the same. A great deal of this training will closely parallel that contained in the avalanche training presented in Chapter 13.

The two most essential elements in disaster search will be *motivation* and *control*. The most difficult task will be to develop and maintain a good working balance between the two.

Motivation

Motivation must be extremely high and can best be gained by excited games of tug-of-war with much enthusiasm and voice encouragement on the part of both the handler and the "victim." Retrieving games are usually not recommended since, in the midst of unstable and hazardous debris, retrieves would be difficult and even dangerous for the dog. Food reward is even more undesirable. Although in disaster training you could set up a short problem and regulate food reward with a predetermined hunger period, in the real situation there would be tremendous drawbacks. During an actual mission, you will be less able to regulate the dog's appetite. Additionally, there are often numerous food items scattered throughout the debris that could be tempting to a dog conditioned with food reward.

Motivation may be heightened by confining the dog (in a crate, on a leash, etc.) until it is actually time to work. The animal will then associate the job at hand with freedom and the opportunity to be with its handler.

Control

Control is essential in disaster work and critical from a safety standpoint. It can and should be taught in several disciplines prior to and in conjunction with search training. General obedience training serves as a basis for all control. Directed search has been mentioned before in wilderness training and may be taught quite easily even in play sessions (as the dog runs after the toy or stick, the handler waves an arm in that direction). As with all training, timing and consistency will be the keys to success. If the handler is clever enough to engineer a successful hit of scent once the dog has followed a given signal and moved away as directed, the dog will soon learn to rely on the assistance of the handler for a more rapid find and the subsequent reward.

The slow nose-to-ground search, using the "seek" or "look" command, will also aid control. Frequent, strategically placed victims and reward sessions are essential for success with this method. This type of work is often utilized in collapsed-structure search as the dog teams are deployed on the top and sides of rubble piles.

Dogs must learn to handle the unstable footing of a large debris pile.   *Irwin Brussel-Smith*

Above all, control must be emphasized in agility training. In addition to the usual obstacle course, dogs should be worked on simulated debris piles, boulders, etc. It is most important to disaster training that the dog regard the agility exercises as exciting and fun *prior* to actually hiding someone within a site and asking the dog to search. The dog should be eager to meet the various challenges, and subsequently rewarded with great enthusiasm. Always remember: you are a team. The dog should learn that it can and must rely on you for direction and physical assistance. If you severely frighten the dog early in the training process, you will find it difficult, if not impossible, to develop a truly reliable disaster search dog.

DISASTER SEARCH TRAINING

Advanced wilderness search training should precede advanced disaster search training. The scent flow is less complicated and more direct in wilderness search. The dog is able to physically follow the scent cone to the victim, perform the recall/refind and receive its play reward. In disaster searching, this is not the case. However, previous extensive wilderness search training will have ingrained an enthusiasm for searching, so the dog will continue to show eagerness even though it may not be able to actually reach the victim.

On the other hand, agility and very basic disaster search can be introduced early in training. Even young puppies should be shown that people can hide in the most unusual places.

Beginner runaways should be set up as in wilderness search, with the victim hiding upwind at the very edge of a mass of debris or in a small rubble pile (logs, brush, tires, etc.) that is relatively easy for the dog to negotiate. Remember, the dog will be running at this stage, without control, and you do not want the animal injured or discouraged. Start the runaways with the handler as the victim and gradually progress to family and friends. Problems should be short, easy and *always* successful. The jubilant tug-of-war reward must be given immediately. If you do not have victims who are willing to make spectacles of themselves and really get the dog excited, do not work a problem that day. It is especially important in the introductory work that the play reward be as spirited as possible. If the dog can be encouraged to bark as part of the play reward, so much the better (it helps if handlers have worked on this separately using a ''speak'' command).

The next step will be to briefly withhold the actual find and thus the reward. The victim will be very close to the surface, but not immediately accessible to the dog. This will again be a runaway, but when the find is made the dog will be encouraged to dig as well as speak (bark or whine). Digging and scratching are natural and can be promoted if the person handling the dog will make a big display of digging himself using both hands, as the dog would paw, and excitedly asking, ''Did you find him? Show me!'' Especially in the

A beginning disaster problem involves boards leaning against a fence, allowing the dog to easily reach the victim.   *Alice Stanley*

A more advanced problem with dog alerting on person hidden in fifty-five-gallon oil drum (note lid) buried upright in debris pile.   *Bob Snyder*

The desolation of a disaster: ARDA dog searching for victims of the Mount Saint Helens eruption.
Jeff Doran

beginning sessions, always try to preplan the problem so that the material the dog must dig into is giving or readily movable and will not discourage or hurt the dog. Again, ensure success.

Repeat these easy problems periodically throughout the dog's development and during the more advanced work in wilderness search. You will be establishing in the dog's mind the realization that people can hide and be found in rubble and debris, that it is great fun to find them there and it can be even more exciting to reach them by barking and digging.

You may also introduce simple building searches (such as in toolsheds, small garages or empty cottages). These may gradually be expanded to larger structures with several stories. Building and disaster search are very similar and it is good training to combine the two.

Scent often behaves strangely in an enclosed structure. The handler should know the victim's location to be able to encourage and properly reward the dog throughout the exercise. Handlers should experiment with various venting techniques (closing most windows but leaving two or three strategically placed windows or doors open).

Graduating complexity will teach the dog to persevere and work the air scent through to its source. A natural progression must be followed, just as in wilderness and avalanche training. The time between the runaway and release will increase. The subject will at times run out of sight behind the debris. The dog will be introduced to searching for subjects hidden some distance within the debris that must be located using a slow, directed search. And, of course, the hidden subjects will gradually become less familiar to the dog.

While the initial victims will be quite close to the surface and able to immediately reward the dog, later subjects should be buried deep within the pile and inaccessible to the dog. The handler should carry a hidden knotted towel and reward the dog as soon as it has given a proper alert (the victim may be cued to add "Atta girl! Good dog!" enthusiastically from below even though out of the dog's reach).

As in all training, there is no room for negative correction. The motivation must be maintained. If the dog seems confused or disinterested, immediately drop back a step or two to an easier stage. Make sure to introduce each new level of complexity by initially using a familiar victim, such as a family member or even the handler if necessary.

Alerts may or may not be pronounced, depending upon a multitude of factors. The air flow within the debris pile will be the most critical controlling factor. Even when buried subjects are relatively close to the surface, their scent may be held below by vacuum areas and opposing air currents. On the other hand, a subject may be a considerable distance from the dog but the scent may be channeled directly to one surface spot as if through a straw. The dog's alert will depend upon the strength of scent encountered. If the concentration of scent is high, the alert will be accordingly pronounced; if the concentration is low or present only in occasional puffs, the dog's alert will be less strong and very often less obvious to the handler. It is general search practice to have any alerts checked by a second dog before reporting them to the rescue workers.

Two keys to success will be the motivation of the dog and the ability of the handler to read the dog. Each team must train under as many varied situations as possible. The handler should know the search dog's individual reactions and alerts under specific conditions. Ongoing experiments to detect scent flow or transport in varying conditions are crucial to enhancing the effectiveness of the search dog.

In training, as on actual missions, the dog may sometimes indicate that it hears the victim by stopping and cocking its head, etc. Bear in mind, however, that the experienced search dog will alert for both live and dead buried subjects.

Articles (clothing, personal belongings, etc.) may have residual human scent and those buried close to the surface may elicit an alert. Generally, the handler will be able to visually check the alert. As in avalanche search, however, the handler must assess each situation and mark all alerts that cannot be completely ruled out.

Once the dog is performing well in a fairly large site, gradually introduce congestion and contamination. The dog should eventually be able to work around crowds of bystanders and other workers, loud noise, smoke and fumes. Contamination may come from numerous sources, including sewage, dead animals and spoiled food. The dog must be able to indicate multiple victims and readily leave one find to search for another.

The polished disaster dog must be maintained with periodic workouts in as many different and varied sites as possible. The workouts may be short, but must always be highly motivational. As frequently as feasible, the dog team should also participate in general disaster drills with the various search personnel and equipment normally involved in an actual situation. Shared knowledge and mutual training beforehand will ultimately ensure the safety and success of future missions.

15

First Aid for Search Dogs

SEARCH MISSIONS can be dangerous for both dogs and handlers. Just as handlers must know first aid for humans, so they must know how to provide emergency, in-field treatment for their dogs.

Preventive health care is the cornerstone of a long and productive life for your dog. An annual visit to the veterinarian is mandatory, during which the dog must receive a routine physical and any necessary vaccinations. In addition, fecal and blood tests for internal parasites should be performed. Many search dog handlers keep their dogs on heartworm medication year-round as a preventive measure.

While all dogs must be protected against both internal and external parasites, three tick-transmitted diseases deserve special attention: Lyme disease, Rocky Mountain Spotted Fever and tick paralysis.

The primary transmitter of Lyme disease is the common deer tick. Spread of the disease to the dog (or human) requires that the tick feed for some time on the host animal. Therefore, it is crucial that your dog be checked thoroughly for ticks after being in the woods, since early removal greatly reduces the risk of a dog contracting this disease. The simplest method for removing a tick is with either your fingers or tweezers; slowly and gently pull until it is removed. Symptoms of Lyme disease include lameness, joint pain and swelling and possible aggression. Current treatment is with antibiotics, such as tetracycline.

Rocky Mountain Spotted Fever produces symptoms of depression, high fever, skin hemorrhages and rashes, loss of appetite, joint pain, coma and possible death. It is transmitted by the American dog tick and the wood tick. Treatment is with tetracycline.

Tick paralysis is caused by a toxin released by the tick into the dog's nervous system, resulting in symptoms ranging from mild unsteadiness to acute immobilization of all four limbs. Removal of the tick should cure this condition.

To help avoid tick-borne disease, you should apply a protective dip or spray repellent on your dog, including inside the ears, before entering the woods.

EMERGENCY FIRST-AID CARE

Health emergencies involving a dog should basically follow human medical guidelines. Search personnel are required to be trained in human first aid and are thus knowledgeable of the ABC's of first-aid care: *A*irway, *B*reathing and *C*irculation. This is also applicable to animals.

The cardinal rule of medicine is ''Thou shalt do no harm.'' When treating an injured and frightened animal, this applies to both the dog *and* the handler. *All dogs bite!* Regardless of how well you know the injured dog, it should be muzzled, especially if it needs to be carried and is suffering from a painful injury.

The simplest and quickest muzzle is a two-inch wide strip of fabric, cloth, gauze roll, etc., tied around the dog's muzzle with a half-knot on top. Bring the two loose ends under the muzzle, cross them and bring them up behind each ear, tying the ends securely below the crown of the dog's skull. It is a good idea to practice this on your dog so that the procedure becomes routine. A word of caution: If the dog is in danger of vomiting or is having difficulty breathing, a muzzle is contraindicated.

Since first aid for a dog is about the same as for a human, the following first-aid care is presented in a simplified and brief form. Where differences occur (such as CPR and artificial respiration), a more detailed account will be given. As in any subject, comprehensive articles and books are available for those who wish a more in-depth study of the subject.

Basic data about the dog:

Normal body temperature: 101.5°–102.5°F (38°–39°C).
Pulse rate: 70 to 180 beats per minute.
Breathing rate: 10 to 30 breaths per minute.

Artificial Respiration and CPR

As mentioned previously, the ABC's of first-aid care should be followed. To check for respiration, place your cheek next to the dog's muzzle, *look* for the chest wall rising and falling, and *feel* for the air being exhaled. If you are wearing glasses and the lenses fog, this is a good indication that the dog is breathing. To perform artificial respiration, you must first clear the airway of debris, fluids, etc. Cup your hands around the dog's mouth holding the muzzle closed, and blow into the nostrils at a rate of fifteen to twenty times per minute. Be sure to allow the lungs to deflate passively for adequate respiratory gas exchange before giving the next breath.

In a situation where mouth-to-nose ventilation is impractical or impossible, an alternative method is as follows. Lay the animal on its right side, extending the head and neck in a straight line with the spine. Pull the tongue forward. Place both hands on the chest wall slightly forward of the last rib and compress the chest twelve times per minute.

To check for cardiac function, either feel for a femoral pulse inside the dog's thigh or, with the dog lying on its right side, feel for the heartbeat directly behind and in line with the elbow. If there is no palpable cardiac function, appropriate CPR must be initiated.

The heart is most efficiently compressed from side to side in dogs since this is the narrowest dimension of the thorax. Use a flat, spread hand rather than the heel. Lay a large dog (over twenty-five pounds) on its right side on a hard surface and exert compression over the widest section of the rib cage. In small dogs, compress the chest wall *between* your two hands, applying compression directly over the heart. The chest should be compressed at a rate of 80 to 100 compressions per minute. The ratio of respirations to compressions should be about one respiration to every four compressions. Check for a pulse to evaluate the effectiveness of the compressions and check mucous membrane color and refill for adequate oxygenation.

Shock

Shock is a life-threatening situation that develops when the body's cells receive inadequate supplies of blood and oxygen. Causes of shock include decreased blood volume due to hemorrhage, severe stress, infection and/or impaired cardiac function.

Symptoms of shock are varied. They may include weakness and/or unconsciousness; pale mucous membranes; cool skin and extremities; rapid heart rate; weak pulse; shallow, rapid breathing; and poor capillary refill (check the capillary refill by pressing down on the gum until it is white, then release pressure to check for immediate return to pink).

First aid involves maintaining respiration, controlling hemorrhage, keeping the dog warm, positioning its head slightly lower than the body and monitoring the pulse. In *all* first-aid emergency situations, anticipate shock and be prepared to treat it.

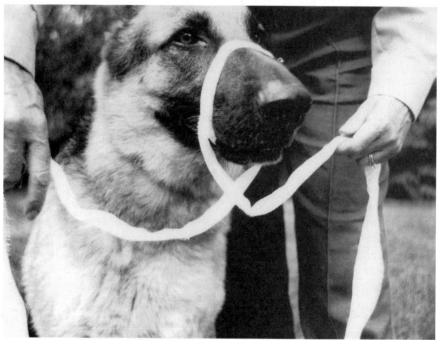

Applying a muzzle:
Step 1: Tie a half-knot over the bridge of the dog's muzzle.
Step 2: Bring both ends under the chin, crossing them.

Step 3: Bring the crossed ends up either side of the dog's head behind the ears and tie securely.   *Heidi Ludewig*

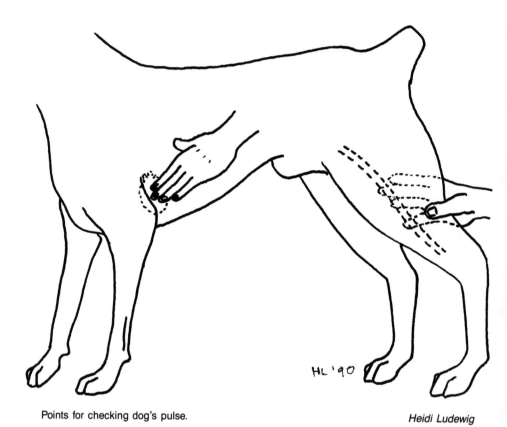

Points for checking dog's pulse.

Heidi Ludewig

Fractures

Signs of an apparent fracture include pain, swelling, grating (sounds of friction between bone fragments), diminished function, abnormal angulation between joints and abnormal movement. Treatment should prevent further injury and make the dog more comfortable. When splinting, the objective is to immobilize the break, using any reasonable material (for example, rolled-up newspapers or magazines, wood, cardboard). Pad the break with cotton or cloth, place the splint around the break and secure it with tape, cloth, rope, etc. Immobilize the joints both above and below the fracture site. Another effective splint that will reduce or prevent swelling is a modified Robert Jones bandage (one with heavily padded splinting material; see illustration on page 188).

Dislocation

Signs of a dislocation include pain, swelling, abnormal joint function, abnormal joint position or angulation and apparent shortening of the limb. First aid is primarily aimed at keeping the dog as comfortable as possible, since correction of the dislocation usually requires general anesthesia.

Open Wounds and Hemorrhage

Open wounds include abrasions, incisions, lacerations and punctures. First aid is to control hemorrhage, either by direct pressure/bandage, cold compresses or a constricting band, and to prevent further trauma and/or contamination of the wound. Once bleeding is under control, clean the wound with an antibacterial soap, hydrogen peroxide, or flush with clean water. When bandaging a limb, wrap *from* the extremity *toward* the body.

A constricting band should be applied tightly enough to stop or slow bleeding, but you should still be able to easily slip a finger beneath it. The band should be slowly released for one minute of every ten minutes applied and then retightened only if necessary.

If a true tourniquet needs to be applied to control bleeding (as in complete avulsion of a limb or body part), realize that you are risking loss of that limb to save the life of the dog. Never release a tourniquet once applied except under orders from a veterinarian (attach a note to the tourniquet recording the time it was applied).

When searching a disaster site where broken glass, wires and other sharp and potentially dangerous rubble abound, it may be advisable to tape the dog's feet. However, the dog will lose some traction and you must weigh the pros and cons of taping or applying booties.

Insect Bites and Scorpion Stings

First aid includes removing the insect and/or its stinger, applying cold compresses (or wet compresses of sodium bicarbonate paste, soothing lotion,

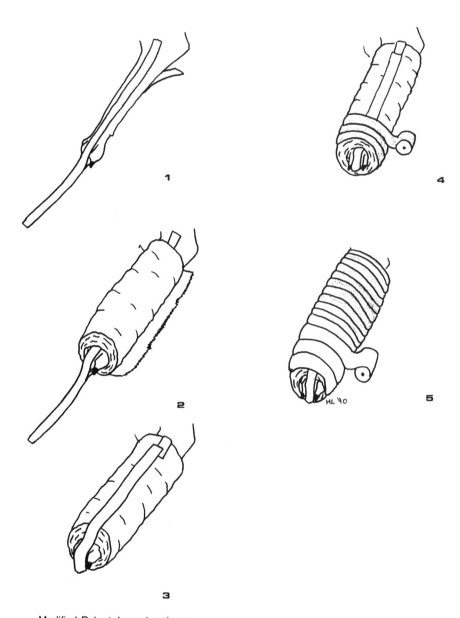

Modified Robert Jones bandage:

Step 1: Apply two pieces of adhesive tape to limb as shown, extending the pieces forward of toes a distance equal to length of the limb.

Step 2: Wrap the taped limb in several layers of roll cotton.

Step 3: Bring the tape stirrup over the cotton.

Step 4: Firmly wrap with elastic wrap or gauze bandage, securing the tape stirrups to the bandage.

Step 5: Complete by applying adhesive wrap (toes left exposed to facilitate checking for limb circulation).

Heidi Ludewig

etc.) and administering oral antihistamine. In severe reactions, apply ice packs to the affected area. If the bite is on a limb, bandage firmly between the swelling and the body to prevent spread of the toxin and seek professional help immediately.

Snakebite

Although snakebites are rarely fatal, tissue damage can be extensive. The general consensus at this time regarding first-aid treatment for snakebite is to subdue and immobilize the dog as much as possible to reduce the uptake of venom into the animal's system and to transport the dog to a veterinary hospital immediately. It is felt that applying constricting bands or attempting to suck the venom from the wound often does more harm than good. If a member of your unit is qualified, intravenous administration of fluids, sedatives and antivenin may be considered. Follow treatment with broad spectrum antibiotics and monitor closely for twenty-four hours.

The severity of snakebite envenomation varies, depending upon the time of year (highest in the spring), the time since the snake last bit, age of the snake (young snakes have high peptide fractions), aggressiveness and motivation of the snake.

Penetrating Objects

Never remove any object penetrating the eye, chest or abdominal cavities. Protect the site of such wounds from further damage and seek professional help. Leave the object in place, supporting and protecting it with bandage wraps.

In other cases, if the penetrating object can be removed *safely* and *easily* without hemorrhage and further damage to the tissues, this should be done and the wound treated accordingly. Special cases:

Porcupine quills: These quills have a hollow interior. When the quill is squeezed (prior to removal) the displaced air forces the quill to expand, which in turn causes the barbs in the skin to expand. Consequently, quills should be cut in half before attempting to remove them; they should then come out quite easily.

Briers, foxtails, etc.: Always examine your dog carefully after being out in the field. Thorns, briers, etc., should be removed before they can imbed themselves in the skin and become a potential site for infection. Take care to examine between the toes and paw pads, and inside the ears.

Burns

First aid for burns involves preventing further damage and helping to reduce pain. Prevent self-injury, flush chemical burns, apply cold compresses and, if aid is delayed, apply a dry or saline bandage. Treat for shock.

Dog being carried after having been bitten by rattlesnake.

Penny Sullivan

When working in hot weather, dogs must be allowed to cool off frequently.

Penny Sullivan

Frostbite

The clinical signs of frostbite may include redness, paleness or scaliness of the exposed tissues. Treatment involves carefully rewarming the tissues by immersing the area or wrapping it with towels soaked in *lukewarm* water. Never rub or massage. Prevent self-injury. To protect your dog's feet against frostbite, you may wish to apply protective tape bandages or purchase booties.

Heatstroke

Symptoms of heatstroke, or hyperthermia, include elevated rectal temperature, rapid pulse, bright red mucous membranes, weakness, shock and collapse. First aid involves reducing the dog's core temperature as quickly as possible by spraying or immersing the dog in cool water and removing it from the sun and heat. Take the dog's temperature every five minutes and discontinue treatment as soon as it returns to normal, then dry the dog to prevent hypothermia.

The most common cause of hyperthermia is leaving a dog unattended in a closed or only partially ventilated vehicle. On a search mission, the dog may need to be left alone while the handler is away (for example, during a briefing). It is highly recommended to crate train or tie your dog outside rather than leave it in a car.

While searching, always carry adequate water for both you and your dog and take frequent water breaks. It is also recommended you allow the dog to swim or lie in a stream when the opportunity presents itself in the field.

Hypothermia

Symptoms of hypothermia include subnormal body temperature, shivering (which will discontinue as the dog continues to lose body heat), decreased pulse rate, weakness, unconsciousness and shock. First aid is aimed at raising the dog's core temperature as quickly as possible; caution must be used, however, as rewarming too rapidly can induce shock or cardiac arrest. Rewarming can be accomplished by immersing the dog in a warm water bath or wrapping it in blankets and towels soaked in warm water. If the dog is fully conscious, you can also administer warm liquids. As in hyperthermia, monitor body temperature and discontinue treatment when the temperature returns to normal. Be careful to avoid burning the dog when rewarming!

Gastric Dilation

Commonly, and inappropriately, termed "bloat," this emergency situation arises when the stomach rapidly fills with gas. A further complication is torsion or volvulus, when the stomach or intestines twist. Symptoms include abdominal distention, difficulty in breathing, possibly cyanosis and shock. First aid involves keeping the animal calm, passing a stomach tube if possible (do not force; there may be torsion) to relieve the distention and transporting *immediately* to a hospital.

To help prevent gastric dilation give frequent, small meals rather than one large one. Do not feed large meals before beginning physical activity and, when in the field, encourage your dog to take small, frequent drinks rather than filling up all at once.

Drowning

Unless you can lift your dog and hold it suspended by the hind limbs for fifteen to thirty seconds to drain fluid from the lungs, lay it on a sloping surface (head lower than the rest of the body) to allow for passive drainage. Check for respiration and cardiac function and begin appropriate first-aid care. Complications following resuscitation include possible lung damage and infection. The dog should be closely monitored for forty-eight hours after initial resuscitation, either at a veterinary hospital or at home, to watch for potential problems, including signs of pneumonia.

To reduce the risk of such an accident, consideration should be given to the use of dog life preservers, tether lines, removal of collars, etc., depending upon water conditions.

Poisoning

Treatment for poisoning depends upon the toxin ingested. Generally, if the poison was not caustic, induce vomiting by administering orally hydrogen peroxide or syrup of ipecac. If the toxin was caustic or corrosive, do not induce vomiting but dilute it with milk or vegetable oil mixed with activated charcoal or kaolin. If it was a known acid, administer antacids such as milk of magnesia or baking soda. If it was a known alkali (base), administer vinegar or lemon juice. First aid is primarily aimed at reducing the amount of ingested poison absorbed by the body. If available, read any labels to find the recommended antidote. Transport the dog immediately to a hospital, advising the staff in advance of your imminent arrival. Poison control center numbers should be readily available.

Diarrhea

The causes of diarrhea are varied, including giardia (a type of protozoa often present in the raw, untreated water search dogs drink), internal parasites, viruses, nerves or digestive insufficiencies. Generally, if the diarrhea only lasts a day or two, restricting or curtailing food intake for a period of twenty-four hours followed by a bland diet of chicken or beef with rice will bring it under control. In all other cases of chronic or prolonged diarrhea, seek veterinary aid to determine its cause. Prolonged bouts can cause severe dehydration and debilitation.

Skunk Odors

Occasionally, search dogs encounter skunks and are sprayed. Remedies for the odor include dipping the dog in tomato juice or herbal douches. A product named Outright, produced by the Bramton Company, is very effective against this problem. Take care to thoroughly flush the sprayed dog's eyes and be aware that its searching abilities may be severely affected for several hours.

Spinal Injuries

The symptoms of a possible spinal injury include pain (which can be severe) in the neck or back, an arched back, reluctance to climb stairs or jump onto an elevated area, weakness, paralysis and/or lack of feeling in the limbs. Objectives of first aid include keeping the dog as immobile as possible, especially in severe cases of spinal trauma where movement might cause spinal cord injury. Transportation should be accomplished in a manner comparable to moving a human suspected of having spinal cord injury. Maintain the dog's position and stabilize its neck (a large cervical collar for humans might fit some of the larger search dogs). The dog should be carefully transported on a rigid surface. Remember the ABC's of first-aid care and treat for shock.

FIRST-AID KIT

The following should be maintained in a dog first-aid kit, to be kept in the base camp:

- Activated charcoal
- Adhesive tape
- Antibiotic ointments (topical and eye), sprays, powders and soap
- Bandage scissors
- Cotton-tipped applicators
- Dacriose or other eyewash
- Disposable razors (to clip hair)
- Ear flush
- Elastic bandage (Ace or similar)
- Hydrogen peroxide
- Kwik-Stop styptic powder
- Large butterfly closures

- List of emergency numbers (twenty-four-hour veterinarian, poison control centers)
- Milk of Magnesia
- Nail clippers
- Oral antibiotics
- Oral antihistamines
- Pain relievers (buffered aspirin, Ascription A/D)
- Pepto-Bismol/Kaolin/Kaopectate
- Pliers/wirecutters
- Roll cotton (cast padding, etc.)
- SAM splint(s)
- Snake antivenin
- Sterile pads/compresses (gauze or Telfa pads)
- Stomach tube
- Thermometer (rectal)
- Tourniquet
- Tranquilizers
- Tweezer/hemostat
- Two-inch bandages (Kling, Webril, Vetrap)

16

ARDA Searches

THE FOLLOWING are accounts of some memorable ARDA searches.

MISSING HIKER

The ARDA was requested to aid in a search for a hiker missing four days in mountainous terrain. Arriving too late to search that day, the unit bivouacked at the 7,500-foot level on Mount Adams.

Because other resources had been exhausted during the first four days of the search, only the ARDA unit was left to carry on the search. The twenty-year-old hiker had been missing five days and four nights, with little hope of survival left. Unit members spent the night considering the search and tactics applied, calculated where they thought the subject should be and planned the next day's search.

The following morning two dog/handler teams were dispatched to the prime area and within three minutes the victim was found alive, after five nights and six days, suffering from exhaustion and hypothermia. He had traveled a creek drainage off the mountain for six and one-half miles. His clothing was badly torn and he had left many of his belongings as he followed the drainage. After examination, food and reassurance, he was released to a Forest Service headquarters.

LOST PROSPECTOR

An ARDA unit was requested to aid in the search for a prospector who was nine days overdue. The sheriff's department had mounted a massive search with no results and wanted to use dogs in a last effort to find the man.

The Civil Air Patrol was conducting practice searches when the call was received, making fixed-wing aircraft readily available. An actual mission was declared, allowing two of the aircraft to be used for transporting the dog teams. After arrival and a quick briefing, the handlers and dogs were transported by four-wheel drive vehicles to the prospector's pickup truck, which was parked on the side of a mountain.

The dog teams were deployed to search the sides of the canyon toward the summit. Approximately four hours into the search, a handler reported a find; unfortunately, the subject was deceased.

The prospector had apparently fallen, broken his leg, tried to stand and had fallen again to his death. Sadly, he had the supplies he needed to survive, but had not used them.

MISSING ELDERLY MAN

A seventy-six-year-old man was missing from his home in a rural, wooded neighborhood. Reportedly in good physical condition, he took long daily walks of up to several miles. He was last seen by a local resident as he walked along a road within a quarter mile of his home. The area had been searched by foot, horseback, helicopter and Bloodhounds.

Two days after his disappearance, an ARDA unit was requested to join the search. The unit's efforts concentrated on roads, driveways and the areas adjacent to them. Within an hour, a team working a heavily wooded section had an alert. The dog left the handler and moments later returned with an indication of a positive find. Following the dog through heavy brush, the handler heard the subject's voice before actually seeing him.

The man had fallen under barbed wire along an old stone wall, just yards away from a well-used bridle path ridden by searchers that same day who had failed to see him due to the heavy underbrush. The man had spoken to the dog as the handler approached, but lapsed into semiconsciousness as a result of hypothermia. Members of the Morristown Intensive Care Unit were on scene in minutes, where they stabilized the subject for transport to a local hospital.

HOMICIDE

The state police requested the aid of an ARDA unit in locating the body of a man who had been missing and presumed dead for four months. The problem presented by the time lapse was compounded by the terrain, which included a semiarid area near a river where only scant moisture had fallen since the victim had disappeared.

ARDA handlers prepare to board helicopter for search that led to recovery of elderly subject alive after being lost several days in woods. *Emil Pelcak*

The unit decided to begin their search at the intersection of a highway and a dirt road, which was the most likely point last seen. In a very short time, one of the dogs alerted on an area approximately seventy-five yards from base camp. The other two handlers responded to that site where, as if on signal, all three dogs began to dig and whine. Authorities began digging and discovered the subject's left foot at a depth of about eighteen inches.

This search served as a reminder that all searches should begin at the base camp boundaries, not a half mile down the road!

MISSING DEAF-MUTE SUBJECT

The ARDA was requested to assist in searching for a seventy-two-year old female who was deaf, mute and diabetic. She had last been seen behind her house at 4:00 the previous afternoon, heading into the woods to find her husband, who had gone to chop wood.

Three dog/handler teams and a base operator responded and, after the initial interviews and review of the map, began searching the woods and maze of logging trails around the woman's house.

One handler had nearly completed his sector when his dog made a pronounced alert but lost the scent near the sector boundary. The handler finished his sector and radioed base he was going to conduct a hasty search of a logging road that was beyond the sector boundary and in the general area of the alert. As he was walking along the road, the handler saw his dog in the distance, approaching what appeared to be a large stump. When he got closer, however, he realized that the top part of the "stump" was the woman, sitting and tapping her walking stick. Through sign language, she let her rescuers know that she had been walking in circles and wanted to go home. Despite being diabetic and spending the night in the woods, she was in good shape and able to walk back to her house.

SKELETAL REMAINS

This incident was not a search, but a unit workout. A light brush problem was planned for a unit trainee. As it was her first long problem, an experienced handler went along to provide guidance. In addition, the trainee's mother was visiting from California and she, too, was trudging along behind as the dog started to work on the "find" command.

The problem was going very well when, after about forty-five minutes, the dog gave an alert. At first the object indicated by the dog did not look like anything special, just a stick on the ground. As the unit members approached, however, it took on definite form. The dog had alerted on a human skull with what appeared to be a bullet hole in the back of the head.

The authorities were notified and, upon their arrival, the area was roped off. At the request of the FBI, the unit returned to the site and subsequently found leg and pelvic bones. The body parts were identified as having come from four different individuals, all homicide victims.

This find pointed out two things: all workouts are not routine and check out every alert your dog gives—you never know what you will find.

LOST CHILD

The ARDA's assistance was requested in the search for a missing two-year-old child who had disappeared along with his three dogs.

Two dog/handler teams responded immediately, with a third scheduled to respond as soon as possible. The two handlers began a hasty search of the roads and paths around the boy's home. They met at an abandoned railroad line, where they found a sandy area containing small footprints and dog tracks. The two handlers split, with each walking a different direction along the railroad in an attempt to find more tracks.

The third handler had arrived and one of the handlers walking the railroad noticed the bright orange parka in the distance as that handler walked to meet him. At the same time, he noticed a brown flash cross the tracks between him and the other handler. The animal appeared too small and dark to be a deer and he assumed it to be one of the child's dogs. He continued toward that point, which was in the middle of a large swampy area that appeared difficult for a small boy to cross. When he reached the point where he had seen the animal cross the rail line, he took his dog into the woods, through water that averaged six inches deep. As he walked he called the child's name—and was surprised to hear a feeble answer. The railroad had been upwind of this side of the woods, but when the child answered the dog also alerted and led the handler to the boy. He was soaking wet with his stocking cap pulled down over his eyes, sobbing and calling for his mother. He was more than a mile from home.

HOMICIDE

The ARDA was asked to search an area near Cairo, New York, for a woman employee of IBM who was feared to be a homicide victim. The woman had last been seen leaving work two weeks earlier. A man wanted in connection with the murder of a Westchester County police officer had been arrested in Toronto, Canada, while driving the missing woman's car. A woman's scalp was found in the car and as a result a search was initiated in a New York area known to be frequented by the suspect. This search led to a burglarized cabin that contained property belonging to the suspect and the missing woman's IBM identification card.

Dog stands on landfill near site of alert on body buried nearly one year.   *Penny Sullivan*

Dog alerts in pile of logs left by force of Mount Saint Helens eruption.   *Jeff Doran*

200

The area around the cabin was searched by police, forest rangers and volunteers for one week without success. The ARDA unit was asked to search the same area and responded with two dog/handler teams.

Despite snow flurries and strong winds, one of the dogs made a strong alert and led his handler to a stone wall. Although it seemed impossible for a body to be hidden in the wall, the handler had strong faith in his dog's reliability and police were called to the scene. Removal of the stones did indeed reveal the scalped body of the missing woman. The suspect had apparently used her scalp as a wig to disguise himself as he crossed the Canadian border. He was later killed by police during an escape attempt.

APPALACHIAN TRAIL MURDERS

A young man and woman hiking the Appalachian Trail were reported ten days overdue. An ARDA unit was requested to assist, responding with four dog teams and a base operator.

The search area encompassed thirty-two miles of the trail and resources included mounted searchers, members of six different rescue squads, the local sheriff's department, state police and Forest Service personnel.

In the afternoon, the dogs began working several miles of trail north of the point where the hikers were last seen. Early that evening, another hiker reported that he had the found the female subject's body, in a sleeping bag hidden under leaves near a shelter north of the original search area. The woman's body was removed, the area sealed off and search efforts suspended until the following morning.

The next morning, three dogs worked the trail leading to the shelter, while a fourth was taken to the site where the female's body had been found in an effort to locate evidence. While searching near the body site, the dog being used to look for evidence gave a pronounced alert and led her handler to a wooded hillside more than 100 feet away. The dog's strong alert and the sight of a freshly broken branch at the base of the hill caused the handler to request accompaniment from the investigating team before proceeding up the hill. A short time after their arrival, the dog indicated a large log at the top of the hill. The male subject's body was found behind it, also in a sleeping bag and covered with logs and leaves. Both subjects had been deceased approximately ten days. The woman had been stabbed repeatedly and the man had been shot in the head three times. Their murderer was subsequently arrested and is incarcerated.

MISSING CHILD

The ARDA was requested to dispatch teams on a search for a two-year-old child. The child had wandered away from the family's mobile home at 5:00 P.M. the previous evening and had not been seen since. Because of the cold night temperatures and the terrain, dog teams were dispatched on an emergency basis.

Four dog/handler teams began searching with the assistance of man trackers as they attempted to determine a direction of travel. Each dog team worked approximately 150 yards ahead of their respective trackers. About an hour and a half into the search the second morning, a unit dog alerted and led its handler to the child, who was lying face down in frozen mud behind a log, nearly a mile beyond what had been described as an "impassable" fence.

The child did not move, even when the handler called to him. As the handler leaned over and touched the apparently lifeless body, the boy suddenly whirled and wrapped his arms around the handler's neck. He did not release his grip during the helicopter evacuation and only relinquished his hold when reunited with his parents. Doctors advised that he was within three or four hours of death when found, but he fully recovered from his ordeal.

LOST HIKER

The ARDA was requested to assist on a search for a hiker who had been missing three months. A large search had been conducted shortly after the man's disappearance, but was suspended due to deep snow and avalanche danger.

Three dog/handler teams responded to the request and began working their sectors. As the dogs worked, a news helicopter flew over and one dog promptly alerted as the downdraft from the helicopter stirred up the air currents. The three dogs continued working and, a short time later, one working higher on the canyon wall also alerted. Shortly afterward, the third dog also alerted and moved uphill to find the hiker's body. The total time elapsed for the search was less than two hours.

LOST BOY

An ARDA unit responded on a search for a missing three-year-old boy. He had last been seen playing in his yard, which was surrounded by forest.

Following the initial interviewing and unit briefing, dog teams began hasty searches along probable escape or funneling routes. Sector searching began at 11:00 that night, with dogs and handlers working through dense, marshy terrain.

Shortly after 1:00 A.M., the search was suspended for the night. One handler decided to finish her sector before returning to base and, as they moved upslope near a natural gas pipeline, her dog alerted. At the same time,

ARDA dog searches building in wake of 1979 tornado in Wichita Falls, Texas. *Bob Koenig*

Dog indicates wall where body of homicide victim was found buried. *Penny Sullivan*

they heard a dog barking and moved in the direction of both the search dog's alert and the barking dog. As the handler flashed her light into the brush, she caught sight of a shiny blonde object under a pine tree. It was the hair of the little boy who was hiding and shivering uncontrollably.

Transported home, he recovered from his ten hours of being lost in the woods.

APPENDIX:

Lost Person Behavior

$\mathbf{T}$HE following are lost-person statistics (distance found from the point last seen) as contained in *Analysis of Lost Person Behavior: An Aid to Search Planning*, by William G. Syrotuck (Arner Publications, 1976). The statistics were based on a total of 229 cases, broken down by state as follows: 117 from Washington State, 95 from New York and 17 from the states of Idaho, Oregon, California, Alaska, New Mexico, Wyoming and Tennessee.

This study did not include extremely mountainous terrain, such as the Rocky Mountains, or desert areas. It primarily pertained to forested areas with level to moderately steep terrain. Each unit must determine their own statistics based on case histories of their region.

CATEGORY BREAKDOWNS

Small Children (one to six years of age, 22 cases)

Toddlers (ages one to three) are usually drawn away by random incidents, such as the appearance of an animal or following a path for the sheer fun of it. They are unaware of the concept of being lost and may travel for hours before deciding "I want my mommy" or feeling alone, tired or hungry. They are likely to remain in the general area and find the handiest place to fall asleep.

Children between three and six are more mobile and have definite interests: finding a playmate, exploring or trying to follow older children. They do have a concept of being lost and usually will make an effort to find a sleeping spot for the night.

The case studies revealed:

Used travel aids: 57 percent. (This percentage used paths, game trails or followed a drainage that afforded a path of least resistance. The remaining 43 percent were found in brushy areas.)

Distances found: within one mile, 38 percent; between one and two miles, 46 percent; between two and three miles, 8 percent; beyond three miles, 8 percent.

Children (six to twelve years of age, 24 cases)

These children have better navigational and distance skills, so are usually well oriented to their normal surroundings. They may wander off to sulk, gain attention or avoid impending punishment. On discovery they are lost, they may be profoundly embarrassed or fearful of possible punishment. At the outset they may be unwilling to answer calls; however, with darkness, cold or other fears they are usually happy to help themselves get found.

The case studies revealed:

Used travel aids: 67 percent.

Distances found: within one mile, 33 percent; between one and two miles, 42 percent; between two and three miles, 17 percent; beyond three miles, 8 percent.

Hunters (100 cases)

The nature of hunting is such that the hunter tends to concentrate more on game than on navigation. The more isolated and rugged the terrain, the greater the likelihood of getting lost.

The case studies revealed:

Used travel aids: 52 percent; the remaining 48 percent were located in timbered or heavily vegetated areas.

Distances found: within one mile, 18 percent; between one and two miles, 47 percent; between two and three miles, 24 percent; beyond three miles, 11 percent.

Hikers (44 cases)

Hikers usually relied on trails and had some destination in mind. Many who have become lost have inadequate maps or none at all and run into problems when trail conditions change. Others are lost when they are mismatched in skills and experience with their companions, resulting in their being left behind and separated from the party.

The case studies revealed:

Used travel aids: 73 percent. Hikers tend to use the path of least resistance.

Distances found: within one mile, 25 percent; between one and two miles, 25 percent; between two and three miles, 25 percent; beyond three miles, 25 percent.

Miscellaneous Outdoor Persons (15 cases)

These comprise a miscellany, mainly adult, of pine cone seekers, berry pickers, mushroom pickers, rock hounds, nature photographers, etc. Generally, the intentions of those in this category are to stay near a road or a particular location. Because their plans are short, they carry no navigational or survival aids. They generally start in good weather and seldom carry spare sweaters or rain gear.

The case studies revealed:

Used travel aids: 30 percent; 70 percent were found in the terrain that occupied their activities.

Distances found: within one mile, 22 percent; between one and two miles, 41 percent; between two and three miles, 11 percent; beyond three miles, 23 percent.

Elderly Persons (above 65 years of age, 24 cases)

Older persons who are senile or suffering from Alzheimer's often pose the same supervision problem as small children and are easily attracted to something that strikes their fancy; more active senior citizens are likely to overextend themselves and suffer a heart attack or exhaustion with a fatal outcome.

The case studies revealed:

Used travel aids: 47 percent.

Distances found: within one mile, 57 percent; between one and two miles, 28 percent; between two and three miles, 8 percent; beyond three miles, 7 percent.

Bill Syrotuck